AF380373

"Based on a lifetime of ministry in western Ethiopia and among the Anyuwaa diaspora in North America, Owar Ojulu proposes a culturally appropriate discipleship as a strategy to help the Anyuwaa church reclaim the gospel in their own context. This book can help the Anyuwaa church and US Christian leaders seeking to help their churches become more faithful and relevant to the world."

—**B. Hunter Farrell**, director, World Mission Initiative,
Pittsburgh Theological Seminary

"Discipleship is difficult in any cultural context, but especially with those whose pre-Christian cultural influences continue to permeate every aspect of their worldview. Owar Ojulu's excellent study on practical discipleship is not only for the Anyuwaa church, both in Ethiopia and the Diaspora, but for all who work among people groups who are struggling with the proper balance between their old way of life and their new life in Christ."

—**Larry W. Caldwell**, professor of intercultural studies and Bible
interpretation, Kairos University

"Standing on the bridge between God's word and God's beloved world among Anyuwaa people, Owar Ojulu insightfully traces the touchpoints where the gospel takes distinctive shape. In this work we receive a compelling, urgent, and universal call to discipling; the model that Ojulu has provided for doing so with contextual sensitivity, prayerful partnership, and spiritual hope is a gift to the Anyuwaa church and Christians everywhere."

—**Beth Lindquist McCaw**, associate professor of ministry, University
of Dubuque Theological Seminary

"In this book, Owar Ojulu presents a foundational resource for contextual social research and ministry engagement. His ministry with the Anyuwaa people and the cultural tensions that surround discipleship decisions illustrates the need for both cultural understanding and theological clarity. This work builds up the body of knowledge for ministry work in this region of Ethiopia and for Doctor of Ministry study in general."

—**Steven Trefz**, professor of practical theology, Kairos University

A Practical Discipleship Model
That Fosters Spiritual Maturity

A Practical Discipleship Model That Fosters Spiritual Maturity

Responses to Tradition, Divinities, and Witch Doctors
in the Context of the Anyuwaa Church

Owar Ojha Ojulu

FOREWORD BY
Samuel Deressa

WIPF & STOCK · Eugene, Oregon

A PRACTICAL DISCIPLESHIP MODEL THAT FOSTERS
SPIRITUAL MATURITY
Responses to Tradition, Divinities, and Witch Doctors
in the Context of the Anyuwaa Church

Wipf & Stock
An Imprint of Wipf and Stock Publishers
199 W. 8th Ave., Suite 3
Eugene, OR 97401

www.wipfandstock.com

PAPERBACK ISBN: 978-1-6667-8376-6
HARDCOVER ISBN: 978-1-6667-8377-3
EBOOK ISBN: 978-1-6667-8378-0

VERSION NUMBER 11/08/23

To my late mother,
Ariet Kwöt, (Nyibïcääri)
whose dreams have come to pass!

Contents

Foreword

THIS BOOK, *A Practical Discipleship Model that Fosters Spiritual Maturity*, aimed towards a stronger church by Owar O. Ojulu, is a captivating work that unfolds the remarkable story of the Anyuwaa church and the profound challenges it has encountered in the realms of discipleship, ministry, and leadership.

Anyuwaa is a vibrant ethnic group in Ethiopia, known for their rich cultural heritage and distinct traditions. They reside primarily in the western part of the country, particularly in the Gambella region. The Anyuwaa people have a long history that is intertwined with the complex tapestry of Ethiopian culture. They have their own unique language, also called Dha-Anyuwaa, which is part of the Nilotic branch of the Sub-Sarah language family. Despite the challenges faced by many indigenous languages, the Anyuwaa community takes pride in preserving and passing on their linguistic heritage to future generations.

The Anyuwaa people have a rich cultural heritage that is expressed through their music, dance, and vibrant ceremonies. Music plays a significant role in their society. Apart from their artistic expressions, the Anyuwaa people have a strong sense of community and kinship ties. They have well-established social structures and systems, ensuring solidarity within their communities. Important decisions are often made collectively, highlighting their communal values and respect for consensus.

With a meticulous focus on unraveling the rich tapestry of the Anyuwaa people's religious journey, this book sheds light on the arduous path toward establishing a resilient foundation for discipleship. From its inception, where Christianity was introduced to the Anyuwaa community in the 1950s by devoted missionaries Don and Lyda McClure, to the present-day struggles and triumphs of the church, discipleship among the Anyuwaa is a testament to the enduring spirit of faith and commitment.

The early phases of evangelization were not without their setbacks. The gospel initially sprouted but failed to fully blossom due to the foreign approach employed by the missionaries. However, the resilience and determination of the Anyuwaa people prevailed, leading to a renewed exploration of the Christian faith in the 1990s, coinciding with Ethiopia's change in regime. Yet, as the gospel surged forward, the lack of comprehensive theological education and a solid doctrinal foundation within the newly formed congregations became apparent. This resulted in a dearth of knowledge among believers, rendering them vulnerable to various challenges and causing divisions within the church. The Anyuwaa church became generational, with each wave of adherents lacking the necessary resources for a mature Christian faith.

In *A Practical Discipleship Model that Fosters Spiritual Maturity*, the author confronts these obstacles head-on, presenting an innovative approach that harmonizes the local resources with gospel teachings. By emphasizing the vital importance of incorporating cultural elements into the discipleship process, this book offers a refreshingly new perspective and a framework for nurturing a strong spiritual foundation.

Through vivid narratives and profound insights, the authors artfully illustrate the transformative power of a holistic discipleship model, one that is intricately attuned to the unique cultural context of the Anyuwaa people. As you embark on this journey alongside the Anyuwaa, you will witness the struggles faced by early missionaries and the urgent need for a biblically grounded understanding of the faith. More importantly, you will encounter a vision for a stronger church that can be extrapolated and applied to faith communities across the globe.

I firmly believe that *A Practical Discipleship Model that Fosters Spiritual Maturity* will serve as an inspirational catalyst for critical thinking among church leaders and individuals genuinely invested in the growth and development of vibrant faith communities. The lessons shared within these pages possess the power to foster growth, maturity, and a deeper connection with the divine within any congregation.

Prepare to be captivated by this extraordinary work and allow the Anyuwaa people's journey to ignite your own passion for discipleship and the pursuit of a stronger, more resilient church. May the insights presented in this book resonate deeply within your being and guide you towards a profound transformation in your spiritual journey.

Rev. Dr. Samuel Deressa, PhD

Associate Professor of Theology and the Global South
and Fiechtner Chair for Christian Outreach,
Director of DCO Program
Concordia University, St. Paul

Acknowledgments

THIS IS A TRUTHFUL fact to state that every book produced, regardless of size and content, is the result of arduous endeavor that involved insights and encouragement of individuals involved. As such, this work is no exception! This study project is an upshot of diligence of thoughtful reassurance of churches and individuals both in Gambella, Ethiopia, as well as in my current ministry context of Ebensburg and Colver Presbyterian churches.

The current discrepancy of spiritual practices and imbalance in church growth of the Anyuwaa church demonstrates a lack of understanding of discipleship and materials available for the church to assist new converts in their faith journey. *This project aims to illuminate the Anyuwaa church regarding the nature of this problem that contributes to the incongruity of discipleship and to suggest effective strategies for handling this crisis.* While leaders of the church acknowledge that while there are mass conversions, it is without corresponding growth in the converts, yet no one has pinpointed the cause of the prevailing challenge. Based on rigorous assessment, the book reflects on experiences and reviews historical, institutional, and individual perspectives regarding this situation. This work reviews elements and provides practical advice for further discussion to disclose the best practice and a contextualized discipleship model that can foster spiritual maturity in the form of small group discussions, class presentations, and prayer conferences. It has been an exciting journey throughout the project research.

But as I rejoice, I also accept my limitations. This project grew out of my curiosity and love for the Anyuwaa church. It is my continued endeavor to understand the lack of a sound discipleship model in the Anyuwaa church and identify the problem and with church leaders curb the trend.

My concern and question have been that for the past twenty years, we have seen massive growth in the church, yet there were unsettling practices, such as polygamy, members dealing in witchcraft, sorcery, fear of village gods, etc. There has been lack of resources to train and educate Christians converts. Thus, this project strives to investigate the Anyuwaa church and understand discipleship ministry and approach. Conducting research in Gambella and among the Anyuwaa church in the West has helped us understand the impact of the issue in the larger spectrum.

Personally, I have learned many things beyond my expectations during the project study. Some practices were made known to me, some of which I was not aware of. It has been a challenge to collect primary information due to distance as my project was on the Anyuwaa church in Gambella, Ethiopia, and lack of secondary resources has made this work challenging. Transitioning and change in my ministry context from Hope Christian Ministry among the Anyuwaa Diaspora in Minnesota, to the current cross-cultural ministry in Ebensburg and Colver Presbyterian churches, and the challenge of the coronavirus have created some emotional impacts. Despite all the challenges, I am delighted that with the help of God and the prayers of many, this project has come to its fulfillment.

In this regard, I want to acknowledge and give thanks to my wife, Apay Okello Olok, whose support never departs from my side. She does everything around the house as a loving mother and a hardworking wife. She was the dream of my mother. My mother's wish was for my well-being and that through my education I would afford to pay dowry to acquire a wife. To our children, who make the life of studies less stressful, as playing is in our family dynamic, and support me in my ministry. We are grateful for God's gift of "Goodness," BeenyJwok, born shortly after Easter, 2021.

My grateful acknowledgement goes to Dr. Steve Trefz whose encouragement and relevant comments and criticisms supported me to sculpt my work in a concrete manner. Dr. Larry Caldwell's insights into my unsettled start were the foundation for my continuation and completion of this work. Thank you to the discussion group and interviewees, whose contribution is paramount to the outcome of this work. This includes Rev. Darach Thatha Abwola, Qes. Gilo Nyigori Okoth, Pastor Peter Agwa Ochalla, Pastor Omo Okwori Ochudho, Mr. Ojulu Okach, Pastor Agwa Okogn, Pastor Ojulu Omod, Qes. Omod Obang Oman, Rev. Gilo Gora Agwa, Mrs. Olima Ochik Gota, Rev. Oboya Oman Ochalla, Rev. Carl Templin, and Mr. Oman Ogala Oman.

What could I have done without Martha O'Brien, a partner in ministry and a Christian friend, whose insights have been "eagle-eyes" hovering over my notes and carefully proofreading the text. I am in debt and owe Mrs. O'Brien a great and heartfelt thank-you and appreciation for her continued support throughout my work. Thank you to the reader and everyone who shared experiences and gave me reliable information through group discussion and interviews. "Should I go on? There isn't enough time for me to speak" on the goodwill of many (Heb 11:32 NIV).

I give God glory and praise!

Abbreviations

AECU	Anyuwaa Evangelical Churches Unity
ATR	African Traditional Religion
ANTR	Anyuwaa Traditional Religion
BERC	Bethesda Evangelical Reformed Church
EGBS	East Gambella Bethel Synod
EECMY	Ethiopian Evangelical Church Mekane Yesus
MAF	Mission Aviation Fellowship
PCUSA	Presbyterian Church USA
PL	Plural
RCA	Reformed Church in America
SG	Singular
TEE	Theological Education by Extension

CHAPTER 1

Discipleship among the Anyuwaa

A Journey towards a Stronger Church

Introduction

THIS BOOK IS THE product of years of endeavor and quest to understand the Anyuwaa church and the prevailing challenge of discipleship and overall church ministry and leadership. Christianity came to the Gambella region in the southwestern part of Ethiopia among the Anyuwaa people in the early 1950s through Sudan by the Presbyterian Church, (USA) World Mission. The gospel came to this remote part of Ethiopia through the self-sacrifice of Don and Lyda McClure, of Blairsville, Pennsylvania, USA.[1] The missionaries lived among the Anyuwaa people and evangelized this ethnic group for over forty years. The seed of the gospel they sowed certainly germinated, but many believe that it failed to blossom because the method used was alien to the community.

Missionaries managed to train a few local evangelists and periodically sent them to villages. Yet Christianity remained in the mission stations and natives considered this religion as a

---

1. Partee, *Story of Don McClure*, 237.

trespasser. In disappointment, some evangelists abandoned their faith and went back to their own villages. They were suppressed by the power of the tradition and as a result many of them became polygamists and ashamed of preaching about a god who does not accept polygamists, divorcees, and/or those who consume locally fermented alcohols.

Throughout this period, Christianity became something to be ashamed of and was left for the neglected, the laziest, and for the younger generation in the society. Those who sought medical services would accept Jesus Christ, but only for the time when they were around missionaries at the mission stations. They would abandon their faith when they got back to their respective villages. Christianity and the gospel messages were ignored, and gospel proclamation could not stand in the face of the Anyuwaa tradition and worldviews.

In the early 1990s, with the regime change in Ethiopia, the word of God began to reach many places in the Anyuwaa area. By 1994, there was no region of the Anyuwaa country that was not touched by the gospel movement, except for Cïrö area. New ways of worship were formulated, speaking in tongues was introduced, and the ministry of healing met with great success.

However, these mass conversions lacked *in-depth* biblical knowledge and understanding of the Christian faith. The emerging congregations were insufficiently instructed in knowledge of biblical texts, basic catechism, and the Christian tradition of informed discipleship. Thus, although the new converts were baptized, they were not provided the resources needed to develop a mature Christian faith based on scripture and an understanding of what Christian discipleship entails.

Since there was little opportunity or resources to develop these understandings, the church experienced setbacks in terms of doctrinal foundation and theological understandings. Mass dropout, both from churches and schools, was seen in the following years, and church divisions erupted. Christianity became generational. One generation comes and is replaced by a new church movement. The gospel was preached but not much attention was given to teaching the basic principles of the Bible, and discipleship was not at the core of those movements. Over time, the Anyuwaa church became increasingly unstable and lacked foundation.

Apparently, there was a lack of a biblical discipleship approach that aimed to incorporate local resources and embed them into the gospel teaching. Although church membership grew quickly, many members did not develop a mature understanding of the expectations of that membership. If one were to chart church growth alongside growth in mature understanding, the two lines would be far from parallel: growth in numbers would far outstrip growth in maturity. This trend has continued until this day. Even if much attention has not been given to this matter, it is in this context that the discipleship framework and a better approach need to be attempted.

Context of Study

In the fall of 1999, I had my first exposure to a different environment on my first trip outside of the Gambella region. The church I belonged to at that time, the Ethiopian Evangelical Church Mekane Yesus (EECMY), East Gambella Bethel Synod (EGBS), sent me to Hosanna Theological Seminary for a theological study. Besides the landscape, food, and the weather, I found wide differences between Christianity in Hosanna, among the Hadiya people, and the one we practiced in Gambella.

People flocked to church in the evenings several days of the week for prayers and meditations. Early Sunday mornings adult Sunday school classes were conducted in different formats. Choir groups were inclusive of young and older Christians; offerings and tithes were practiced with dedication. Unlike in Gambella, many marriages and wedding ceremonies were conducted in the churches. In my four years in Hosanna, polygamy was not a question for the church and rarely was practiced among nonbelievers.

I kept thinking of Christian faith and discipleship practices in the Anyuwaa church of Gambella. As part of my inquiry, I continued asking our leaders and a few old missionaries who were still alive at the time. I needed to know how the gospel was first introduced to the Anyuwaa people and why it was different from the one in Hosanna. Among the responses, "Anyuwaa were ignorant and stubborn" punched my guts, but still I acknowledged those missionaries' efforts to evangelize my people.

I was not naive, but as a young person I was ready to explore. After I graduated in 2003, I left Southern Ethiopia and went back to Gambella in the West. I learned that many church leaders in my denomination were aware of the prevailing discipleship issue but ignored the problem. As a team, we began giving training and leading group discussions, trying to help church leaders begin to address discipleship issues.

When I left Gambella, Ethiopia, in 2008, I arrived in Minnesota and made my home among the Anyuwaa in Diaspora for eight years. I had dived into ministry, leading Bible studies as well as language, literature, and youth programs. Yet questions continued lingering in my mind: Why is there amazing church growth but minimal commitment to the teachings of the church? What makes theological understandings shallow in the Anyuwaa Christian church? Could there be any influence from the Anyuwaa tradition, religious practice, and worldview involved? Or could it be lack of embedding the best practices in the Anyuwaa culture and religion into the preaching of the gospel?

As stated above, this project grew out of my curiosity and love for the Anyuwaa church. Since 1997, starting as a lay evangelist, I have been serving the Anyuwaa church in different areas of ministry. It is my continued endeavor to understand the lack of a sound discipleship model in the Anyuwaa church and identify comprehensive efforts of the church leaders to curb this trend. Even though I am currently serving two Presbyterian congregations in the USA, I have strong connections with the Anyuwaa church on both continents. In my fifteen years in America, I have made nine trips to Ethiopia.

I have fresh memories and am still familiar with the discipleship situation in Gambella, Ethiopia. I am part of the church leadership in Gambella—the Bethesda Evangelical Reformed

Church. Every year or so, I travel to Ethiopia to preach and teach, to provide counseling and conduct short biblical trainings for the local church leaders, and to organize spiritual conferences. These connections and constant communication with the leadership on the ground make me aware of the continued prevailing problem. In the Diaspora, I have great relationships with pastors and lay leaders in the USA and Canada, some of who have contributed to this project. It is my belief that this work will shine light on the current issue that is threatening the integrity of the gospel and the value of discipleship in the Anyuwaa church both in Ethiopia and the *Diaspora*. And now that my ministry is among the Americans, the project will somehow blend both practices, consider the outcomes, and utilize what I trust will prove to be a more fruitful approach in the church among the Anyuwaa people all over the world and the universal church of Christ.

Discipleship Crisis Foretold

The discipleship crisis in Africa was predicted in the twentieth century at the first conference held in Eastbourne, England, in 1999, where renowned theologians gathered to discuss the paradox and sought to define a path forward for the church. At the conference, the great African theologian Tokunboh Adeyemo called attention to the discipleship predicament facing the continent of Africa and said, "The Church in Africa, is one mile long, but only one inch deep."[2]

Adeyemo was right. As with churches throughout the world in the twenty-first century, practical and Bible-based discipleship is at stake in the church of Africa and specifically in the Anyuwaa congregations. The Anyuwaa church has failed to teach a sound doctrine guided by a discipleship approach to foster Christian maturity. This differs from the way the original missionaries approached evangelization in the past. The missionaries utilized a method or approach that served to evangelize the small number of the Anyuwaa. Even if

2. "Make Disciples," 28.

many agree that such approach failed in practice, it is true that the missionaries shared the gospel that was pure, authentic, and biblical, but only far from contextualization.

However, the new emerging evangelization is more interested in mass conversion rather than preaching sound doctrine. As a result, church growth is not aligned with Christian maturity guided by biblical teachings. In some areas, syncretism is looming over pure gospel. A biblical approach to morals and ethics is eroding and efforts to adhere to biblical principles are ignored. Yet, an important fact is that new converts need a guided discipleship teaching that helps them toward a better understanding of their faith and knowledge of God. As Dallas Willard said, "Such relationships are not efficient, but they are essential to our growing in grace."[3]

For the past twenty years, we have seen mass dropouts, switching of denominational memberships, and more Christian believers practicing polygamy, dealing in witchcraft, fearing village gods, and electing polygamists for church leadership. There is also a lack of resources to train and educate Christian converts.

This problem needs to be addressed within the church system to help raise strong and faithful believers in the church of God. And practical discipleship seeks to identify the source of the current problem, to encourage continued discussion, and present a practical and effective discipleship approach for the church leaders.

Discipleship fosters a Christian life as a process in the transformation to Christlikeness. This process of transformation in God's knowledge includes strong participation and commitment in the life of the church and individual self-dedication to the teachings of the Bible. Discipleship explores basic Christian beliefs and provides biblical foundation in a sociocultural context to foster mature Christian life. It helps us build faith and trust in the atoning work of Christ, which we receive by faith. This is lacking in the Anyuwaa church, both in Gambella and in the Diaspora.

We can strongly state that the current crisis in the Anyuwaa church is due to a lack of biblical understanding about discipleship

3. Willard, *Great Omission*, 215.

and the failure to recognize and work toward possible change of the whole Anyuwaa church irrespective of denomination.

Therefore, this project identifies the source of the current discipleship crisis, encourages continued discussion, and presents a practical and effective discipleship approach for the church leaders. It explores the lack of spiritual maturity and theological understanding in the Anyuwaa church. Henceforth, we took a critical look into the Anyuwaa traditional religion and how it had contributed to these misguided practices in our church.

The Essence of Discipleship

What is discipleship and who is a disciple? This is an essential question when it comes to the discipleship approach and the process in which a person grows in Christlikeness. In his work *The Great Omission*, Dallas Willard presented a great definition for a disciple. "A disciple is a learner, an apprentice—a practitioner, even if only a beginner."[4] Also In his book *The Radical Disciple*, John Stott diligently defined radical disciples as those who took serious responsibilities to following a teacher and "anybody whose opinions went to the roots and was thoroughgoing in their commitment."[5]

It is irrefutable to state that discipleship is an intentional and continual equipping process of believers to maintain the truth of the gospel while applying contextual elements in a perceptive manner. *Discipleship is a lifelong effort to dive deep into the roots of the mystery of the teachings of Jesus Christ about God, human relationships, and the world.* A disciple is a continual learner. No one graduates from the school of discipleship nor retires from being a disciple of Jesus Christ. Discipleship is a congruity with the master because "knowing God requires cognitive union with him in which our whole being is affected by his love and holiness."[6] This encourages many of us to lead the church. And like others, we keep

---

4. Willard, *Great Omission*, loc. 114.

5. Stott, *Radical Disciple*, 15.

6. Osmer, *Teaching Ministry*, 17.

asking questions and exploring for a better understanding, so we can contribute better to the growth of the church. Whether for better or worse, the Anyuwaa has currently embraced denominational bindings, yet without clear doctrinal and liturgical differences.

Study shows that a majority of the Anyuwaa consider themselves as Christians.[7] But the lingering questions remain: Why is there such growth but such a weak foundation of faith? What is the reason that members switch churches or give up faith in large numbers every year? Are there Christians who are afraid of being bewitched? Or who seeks counsel from witch doctors? Are there Christians who still fear or believe in curses or in village gods? What must be the reason that polygamy is highly practiced in the Anyuwaa church even among devout Christians? Are there areas in which our tradition is affecting our churches both positively and negatively? How many of our churches provide discipleship for their converts? Do we see growth in faithful living among our respective church members? What do we think might be a solution to these issues facing our churches? This project answers these questions and provides biblical foundation, analyzes theoretical insights, and embeds practical theological approaches to assist the church and its leaders in their contemporary discipleship predicaments.

Exploring Discipleship Crisis and Methodology

The above questions explore and explain the cause. And the purpose of the project is to suggest ways and to encourage continued conversation in the Anyuwaa church around discipleship and the benefit of catechisms for new converts. The premise of the research methodology is that oral interviews and group discussions were the main medium to collect substantial information. A group of seven pastors from different denominations in Gambella was part of the study group. While the study group was conducted in person, the

---

7. Central Statistics Agency of Ethiopia, *Population and Housing*, 33–34.

individual interviews both in the USA and Canada were conducted by phone, Zoom, and questionnaire reflections.

Group discussion became a safe space for local pastors to converse as partners and colleagues, and everyone contributed to the discussion. This created a conducive atmosphere where everyone was free and motivated to share and engage in conversation. The individual interviews were also individually oriented. While the interviewee takes the center of the conversation, the researcher played the key role of listening to help capture the substance of the discussion. This method was utilized to convince the interviewee of the interviewer's close attention to the task. This methodology of collecting information from both continents gave us full scope and a better understanding of the effect of the lack of a biblical discipleship approach in the Anyuwaa church.

Again, the project assumed to investigate the overall aspects of the challenges of discipleship and the effect of tradition and divinities that affect the life of the Anyuwaa church. Concerns such as tradition, modernity, and discipleship in the current context are integral to the problems that our church is facing.

Pastors and lay leaders with different age groups, from varied denominations, were open for discussion and interested in engaging in further conversation on the practical discipleship model. Therefore, from a denominational perspective, the project makes a substantial contribution to the whole of Christianity in both Gambella and the Diaspora and helps raise faithful Christians in the kingdom of God.

This statement remains truthful. That practical discipleship approach begins with an overview of discipleship; that *discipleship is a continual development process to intentionally equip believers to maintain the truth of the gospel and apply contextual elements, and it is about God's work through Christ Jesus.*

To understand the cultural context of the Anyuwaa church, the project gives a synopsis of the Anyuwaa pre-Christian and post-Christian religions and their worldview. Tradition gives identity and connection between now and then. As you read through the book, the project looks at the Anyuwaa tradition and religion as it plays a significant role in understanding the past and helps to interpret the present context of the Anyuwaa church. It strives to investigate the Anyuwaa church and understand similarities and differences when it comes to discipleship practices in both Africa and the Americas. The research conducted in Gambella and among the Anyuwaa church in the West will help the readers understand the impact of the issue in the larger spectrum and propose approaches that are applicable in the life of the church and encourage further discussion. Therefore, the book benefits the reader when it is read with sedulous tenderness. The chapters are built congruently. Each chapter is built on the premise of the other and provides substantial, yet applicable knowledge and understanding thereof.

In chapter 1, we explore the context, methodology and the essence of discipleship. Chapter 2 touches on concepts, reconstructs texts from the New and Old Testaments dealing with discipleship ministry, and generally analyzes ecclesiastical endeavor to enhance discipleship ministry both then and now. Additionally, aspects of marriage and idolatry are discussed as assumed contributors to a discipleship approach and attitude in the church. Chapter 3 brings a brief, yet informative history and worldview of the Anyuwaa people toward the discipleship method. It argues the importance of culturally informed disciples as an "effective community of cultural agents."[8] Chapter 4 evaluates the process of the project's challenges and opportunities. You are cordially invited to journey through chapter 5. This chapter presents elements and recommends a constructive approach and the implementation of contextual interpretation of the text of the gospel through the lenses of cultural context. And in conclusion, the readers will absorb elements, best practices, suggestions, and guidelines of discipleship ministry discussed in prior chapters. Finally, I encourage the reader to read the verbatim on appendix II, where the focus group provided great reflection about discipleship crisis in their respective congregations in relation to witchcraft and practice of traditional beliefs and worldviews.

8. Vanhoozer, *Everyday Theology*, 55

Moreover, I am convinced that you, as the reader, will be richly blessed from reading this book. You will find resources that will fit into your faith journey, encourage, and uplift your spirit to continue your walk with God. *This is because a biblical-focused, practical discipleship model that fosters spiritual maturity is both for personal enrichment and corporate endeavor to effectively utilize a contextual discipleship approach and enrichment of faith.* This is the only project that has been done to address this matter in the context of the Anyuwaa community and its church. It delivers the best approach and practice! It suggests ways to amalgamate our gospel preaching with elements from our traditional religion, culture, and practices to foster a better theological understanding of discipleship ministry.

Come let us go! (Mark 4:35 NIV)

CHAPTER 2

Biblical and Theological Foundations of Discipleship Ministry

Old Testament Concept of Discipleship

We are convinced that any attempt to understand and apply a contextual discipleship approach without consulting OT sources is deemed incomplete. The Old Testament sources are the foundation of any credible claim in the New Testament and the history of the church of Christ. This is because the OT has rich resources that support our claims and enrich basic understanding regarding any prerogative assessments and assertions.

As such, throughout the history of the church, there have been many basic understandings and beliefs, agreements, and arguments regarding the Old Testament concept of discipleship. Many argue that the relationship between followers and their masters in the OT does not meet the concept and characteristics of discipleship. They debated that "the teacher-disciple relationship was absent in the

OT because there was only one who was to be revered and whose word was to be followed, the Lord himself."[1]

However, we strongly believe and concur with others who maintained that even if it lacks or rarely uses a terminology that specifically refers to discipleship, the OT has clear evidence that holds the concept of discipleship like the New Testament.[2] It is a rich manuscript that gives us diverse and valid resources for the enrichment of faith and spiritual practices.

For this reason, the OT has been the source of references when we talk about the discipleship ministry and models throughout centuries of the Christian faith. Take the word בְּלִמֻּדָי (*belimmuday*) from לִמּוּד (*lamad*), meaning "with my disciples" in Isa 8:16. This text refers to two things: it refers to teaching and the adherents as disciples. It indicates the responsibility of a disciple, meaning to preserve scrolls (the covenant text) and to keep the principles of the law.[3] It also denotes the concept of a follower-teacher. The word בְּלִמֻּדָי (*belimmuday*), meaning "with my disciples," is stated along with the binding and sealing of the law and instructions as it was transferred by Isaiah as the leader. As John Watts has said, Isaiah had a small circle of followers to whom he informally entrusted, and he "deposited his treasure of warnings and teachings with his disciples."[4]

Isaiah had assembled a small group of disciples to cling to his words and continue to preserve the covenant text of God. Renowned English Bible translations agree on this fact and render the Hebrew word in the same context. They hold the idea of the teacher-disciple relationship concept in their translations: "Bind up the testimony, seal the law among my disciples" (NKJV) or "Bind up this testimony of warning, seal up God's instructions among my disciples" (NIV).

The fundamental idea about encouraging and engaging followers in their spiritual growth, adherence to their masters'

1. Marriner, "Discipleship," para 1.
2. Marriner, "Discipleship," Para 4.
3. "Limmud."
4. Watts, *Word Biblical Commentary*, 122–23.

teachings, and their cooperation with God, is a substantial element in the concept of discipleship. The master-servant or teacher-disciples relationship is contextual to the OT. And the opportunities to transform the identity and ministry of the followers is at the heart of the OT. Those relationships and continued learning have helped to identify new ways of equipping and empowering others for ministry, at the time of judges, as well as when the temple ministry was established.

Samuel established the first school of prophets to train faithful servants. Samuel needed the new recruits to understand the doctrine, theology, and the purpose of God for Israel (1 Sam 19:18–24). That in and of itself is discipleship! It has been identified that discipleship is only effective if conducted in the light of a context—cultural, political, and societal settings. Thus, the understanding of the sovereign nature of God and God's purpose is at the core of the books of the Old Testament.

Discipleship is an organized formal and nonformal system by which the truth of the Scripture, promises, and the purpose of God's covenant are passed on through generations in the history of the Old Testament and the Christian faith. Therefore, it must be clear that the relationships between the prophets and their followers, leaders, and their servants, etc., imply the concept of discipleship and the method to disciple others. We can also go as far back as Genesis and claim that the creation of Adam, the call of Noah and the construction of Ark, and Abraham's invitation to journey with God are all intertwined in God's correlated plan to pass on his divine purpose through a guided discipleship model in a master-servant relationship to foster mutual understanding between the respective parties.

In the light of the above statement, we can strongly claim that God had discipled Adam, Noah, and Abraham, to mention a few. Discipleship involves a call, following, and action, which requires enduring obedient learning to understand the purpose of the caller. In elaboration, discipleship is about heeding the *call (hearing the voice and identifying the caller); following the caller (taking an action to step into the intended partnership); and being obedient to the covenant (commitment and remembrance).*

In this regard, we can strongly argue that discipleship originated with God from the Old Testament—then and now. From Genesis to Malachi and Matthew to the Revelations, we see God actively involved in discipling those whom he had called for his purpose.

In the Genesis account, we learn that after God had created heaven and earth, but when nothing had sprung from the earth, the "Lord God formed man from the dust of the ground and breathed into his nostrils the breath of life; and the man became a living being" (Gen 2:1–24 NIV). As stated above, the first step in discipleship is calling. So, in forming Adam from the dust, which symbolizes destruction, inability, and wretchedness, God was calling Adam and breathing the breath of life into his system. Everything that followed was God discipling Adam. He discipled him how to name things, how to cultivate in God's kingdom, how to differentiate between good and bad, and how to hear God. Then God attended to his needs when he realized that Adam, now a living person, needed a partner who would be the mother of many—Eve. God's ultimate purpose for Adam was to be a trusted disciple, a caretaker of creation, and to multiply humankind. God empowered and covenanted with Adam with instructions in a teacher-disciple relationship.

Likewise, God discipled Noah in an extraordinary fashion by calling him to hew a cypress tree and turn it into a lifesaving ship. Discipleship entails empowering others to take responsibility, to step beyond their incapability, to undertake tasks that seem impossible, and to accept the master's will and sovereignty with courage and trust.

Hewing countless cypress trees seemed impossible for Noah, but God vested in him the ability to form a ship. Then he did everything exactly according to the instructions of the Lord in a discipleship approach. It must also be true that God himself worked on the Ark whenever Noah was resting. As a true disciple, Noah listened to the voice, stepped outside of his circle, and opposed his contemporary cultural trends. He trusted the Lord, and walked toward the great purpose of God to save a human generation through the power of an Ark. "Go into the ark" (Gen 7:1 NIV), the Lord said. Noah did, because through the years of instructions, he understood the identity of God (God's doctrine) and his purpose, which is the foundation and the reason for discipleship (God's theology).

Noah did not cease learning to understand God and God's plan. He did all that God had commanded him (Gen 7:5, 22). He persisted in learning and kept cooperating with God until the end of the flood when he built an altar, worshiped the Lord, and then God made a covenant with him (Gen 6:18; 9:17). Noah knew that in discipleship, we take God at his word and keep exploring his purpose for us. This serves as an analogy of Jesus calling and equipping his disciples to rescue humanity from loss and destruction through the Great Commission.

The story of Genesis changed with the call of Abraham. As our faith patriarch, Abraham is an excellent example when we talk about the concept of discipleship in the OT. The Lord had called Abraham to leave his native country and the people he had known in his life. God's purpose was to make Abraham a new person, a separate nation out of the world of the Chaldeans, and for God to bless Abraham and that Abraham becomes a blessing for others. His call to go and follow where God leads him describes the best relationship between a follower and a teacher. Abraham's obedience draws God to fully disclose God's universal presence, sovereignty, and steadfast love toward every nation of the world (Gen 12:1–8).

We can boldly claim that every hardship Abraham and Sarah had persevered was part of their discernment and discipleship process in God's leadership. God taught him of the miracle by giving them a child after they had passed childbearing ages; God showed his providential care in the provision of the ram hanging in the bush. And God was disclosing his true-self, salvific plan, and his presence to Abraham in renewing the divine covenant.

The relationship between God and Abraham represents the fact that discipleship is both theoretical and practical in nature. It must be clear that for any discipleship method to be effective, it must be carried out based on context. God utilized a contextualized discipleship method as he invited Abraham to present what he had available in his context as a symbol for the covenant reengagement. This model helps a learner to understand better the subject matter.

We read in Genesis that the Lord had asked Abraham to bring him a heifer, a goat, a ram, a dove, and a young pigeon to offer. Abraham did and waited patiently as he was instructed. Truly, "when the sun had set and darkness had fallen, a smoking firepot with a blazing torch appeared and passed between the pieces" of elements (Gen 15:1–21 NIV). God had renewed his promises and re-ratified their covenant using elements Abraham had known in his culture. God showed his presence through the firepot that contained a blazing torch, which represents a symbol of contentment. Thus, Abraham learned all that, he believed it, and became God's friend (Jas 2:23). He was, indeed, a disciple of the Lord Jehovah.

Inherently, that is what we claim as God's contextual discipleship approach, which we are called to emulate in our walk with God. Abraham remained faithful to God's promises and the determination to fulfill them in God's own time (Rom 4:19). His years of discipleship had resulted in a great relationship with God, and he was called God's friend. Is that not the concept of discipleship: to discern, follow God's lead, understand his purpose, make commitments to serve him, and be friends of his? Abraham did that (John 15:14–15).

As stated above, discipleship is the process by which we assist followers to enter God's realm by faith, understand God's characteristics (*doctrine*) and provide an unshakable foundation for our faith (*theology*). We encourage the followers to remember and rediscover the journey and decision they have taken so far. We need to assure them and make them confident that they are disciples who explore God's purpose for the world, the church, and for themselves.

Therefore, to delineate God as teacher and discipleship as his, it is not only appropriate recognition, but it is a firm understanding of the truth. It is a noble perception to hold that God speaks and shows us the way and then we carry out his purpose of being for others like Abraham.

Also, discipleship is the practice of *equipping, sending, and acting.* In action, a disciple is compelled to convey the message with which he or she is entrusted. We see this concept of discipleship in the call and sending of Moses. When he had most of his questions answered, Moses was discharged to convey the message of deliverance of Israel from dust and destruction of Egypt to journey in a new life with God like Adam (Exod 7:16). Moses acted as a missionary for the Lord. When Moses had doubts, God discipled him how to utilize his staff. When he was perplexed, he was encouraged to pick up the staff and instructed to do the same when he would approach Pharaoh (Exod 7:10). What he had was an ordinary staff, but the Lord turned that into a tool to witness God's sovereignty and might throughout the journey including crossing the Red Sea and throughout the wilderness (Exod 14; Num 20:11). This suggests that our response to our call to discipleship is grounded in and connected to our social identities and best cultural practices that are rooted in shared stories. It represents a contextualized approach to the discipleship process, as such as that of Jesus in the New Testament (Matt 15:34; Luke 24:41–42; John 21:4; etc.)

A disciple is a "follower, or adherent of a teacher or religious leader."[5] Therefore, it must be clear that most of the relationships between leaders and their followers in the Old Testament justify the concept and fulfill the qualities of a teacher-follower discipleship relationship. These includes Moses' acceptance of Jethroe's advice, his relationship with the community leaders he had trained (Exod 18), and his relationship with Joshua (Deut 31:7–8; 34:4; Exod 24:13); the call of Elisha (1 Kgs 19:19–21) and his relationship with Elijah (2 Kgs 2); and Eli and Samuel (1 Sam 3), prophets and their followers, etc.

5. Freedman et al., *Eerdmans Dictionary,* 348.

We strongly claim that the whole spectrum of God's relationship with Israel is also profound evidence of an effective relationship of teacher and follower, evidence of discipleship in the Old Testament (Hos 11:3–4; Isa 42:6; 49:6).

The Concept of Marriage and Divinities in the OT

1. Marriage, Divorce, and Polygamy

The issue of marriage, divinities, and aspects of cultural attributes are part of the discipleship process. One cannot talk about discipleship without analyzing matters of culture, tradition, and worldviews to acquire a better understanding of the context. When we begin a conversation about marriage, we are also compelled to touch on divorce and polygamy, as they are inseparable matters. But one may ask, what is marriage? Marriage has a deep meaning, which sourced from God. Far from our current cultural perceptions and views, the Old Testament holds that marriage is a sacred covenant bestowed on and between a man and woman.

The purpose of marriage is to symbolize God's unity and partnership between the couples (Gen 2:24). It is an earthly illustration of our spiritual intimacy with God (Ezek 16:8).[6] Marriage holds an element of spiritual worship, divine and trinitarian correlation. In their union, the couple are encouraged to persist in learning, define their purpose, and claim their future with God.

We learn that the Mosaic law suggested divorce (Deut 24:1–4) and Ezra directed the Jews to divorce their gentile wives whom they had married during their exile (Ezra 10:10–11). In this regard, when the Pharisees questioned and wanted to support their argument, Jesus' response was profound: "It was because you were so hard-hearted that Moses allowed you to divorce your wives, but from the beginning it was not so" (Matt 19:8 NRSV).

In this reference, Jesus made it clear that it was Moses, not God, who allowed them to follow their desires. Moses did so after being perturbed as Israel desired to follow the customs of their

6. Christian Families Today, *Living Jesus*, 65.

surrounding tribes (Deut 20:18). We see a similar incident when they wanted to have a king over them. Samuel refused and strongly argued that Israel had God as king over them. Yet, the Israelites were furious and determined to have a human king over them, demanding, "So that we also may be like other nations, and that our king may govern us and go out before us and fight our battles" (1 Sam 8:10–20 NIV). Then Samuel appointed Saul as king over them as they had asked (1 Sam 10:1).

Therefore, the Samuel text serves as evidence that humankind's wishful desires, the hardening of hearts, and failure to understand God's purpose in marriage were the causes for allowing divorce. However, divorcing a partner is "a matter of grave seriousness and is always treated as such in the OT and NT."[7] According to the law of Deuteronomy, a man was prohibited from remarrying a woman whom he had previously divorced. Since the law did not specifically prohibit divorce in other circumstances, the Israelites took for granted that divorce in other circumstances was permitted. It was in essence "to make divorce so solemn and final that it would not be entered upon lightly."[8]

We need to understand that God objects to divorce in the Old Testament and the AMP includes a remarkably effective translation to help us understand the Malachi's passage in simple terms:

> And did not God make [you and your wife] one [flesh]? Did not One make you and preserve your spirit alive? And why [did God make you two] one? Because He sought a godly offspring [from your union]. Therefore, take heed to yourselves, and let no one deal treacherously and be faithless to the wife of his youth. For the Lord, the God of Israel, says: I hate divorce and marital separation and him who covers his garment [his wife] with violence. Therefore, keep a watch upon your spirit [that it may be controlled by my Spirit], that you deal not treacherously and faithlessly [with your marriage mate]. (Mal 2:15–16 AMP; brackets in the original)

7. Freedman et al., *Eerdmans Dictionary*, 351.

8. McConville, "Deuteronomy," 221.

This passage discloses God's intention for our earthly marriages. The relationship between God and Israel has often been referred to as marriage with God, and divorce as rejection of God's covenantal leadership. And faithfulness in marriage reflects God's steadfast love for his people (Hos 2:19). And the love of God in the figurative marriage of Hosea conveys the promise of restoration and the will to renew the covenant and realign the position with God during the return to God (Jer 4:1; Hos 3:5; 14:1).

Therefore, it is a noble position to hold that the Old Testament perception of divorce and of polygamy is as of the New Testament; and marriage is a symbol of inseparable union with God-self.

Regarding polygamy, nowhere in the Bible do we read of God's instituting and ordaining the marriage of multiple wives. It was not part of God's design and did not come from him. Like divorce, polygamy comes as the result of lust, perversion, and lack of self-control. Genesis 4:19, where we first encounter a case of polygamy, appears as evidence of the increase of human transgressions, iniquity, and sins. And the consequence of polygamy from the beginning was chaotic, filled with terror, death, and separation. Sin increased (Gen 6:11–13); families were divided (Gen 21:8–2); curses fell on the families (2 Sam 13:1–39); and the unified kingdom of Israel dissolved (1 Kgs 11, 12), only to mention a few.

Therefore, it is an obvious truth and perceptible for all of us that God does not allow premeditated divorce and never ordained polygamy. His purposes for us are to reflect his will and remain true to him in our earthly marriages as a symbol of our indispensable partnership with God.

2. *Divinities, Divinations, and Witchcrafts*

The existence of other gods, the practice of divination or sorcery, and witchcraft are important subjects in the Old Testament accounts and theology. The OT has recognized the existence of other gods that are presented in the forms of crafted idols.

Our first encounter was from as early in the story of Jacob, Laban, and Rachel (Gen 31:19–35). The first of the Ten Commandments is the acknowledgement of the existence of other gods in different forms in the world—"You shall have no other gods before Me" (Exod 20:2–17 NKJV).

We come across similar claims and instructions of God throughout the OT. In essence, it is the language by which the Lord speaks to his people, admonishing them to abide in him, and to follow his ordinances rather than worshipping or revering human-made gods. This is because Israel has been shown the hand of God; they should know and understand that "the Lord is God [doctrine; and] there is no other besides him" (Deut 4:35 ESV). And Israel is called to be God's witness and servant that may know and understand God's divine plan (Isa 43:10).

This has been a recurring position of the OT, that apart from the almighty God, there is no other god (Isa 45:55). As in the words of Jacob, Israel is summoned to get rid of the foreign gods among them, to purify themselves, and to change their clothes of old self to enter to a new and transformed family of God's household (Gen 35:2). This proclamation of Jacob serves as a *principle for discipleship as it calls to newness and pledges allegiance to the Lord God.*

Like divinities, the Old Testament Bible also has mentioned in many places the existence of diviners, the practice of divination, and sorcery. The first known diviner was Balaam, whom Balak summoned to cast a curse upon Israel but failed (Num 22–23) and later was put to death by Joshua (Josh 13:22).

As the Lord is against any worship of other gods, God strongly warned his people against the practice of divination, witchcraft, and sorceries. God hates such practices, and it is against his divine will and authority.

"The nations you will dispossess listen to those who practice sorcery or divination. But as for you, the Lord your God has not permitted you to do so" (Deut 18:14 NIV). Rejection of such instruction leads to cutting ties with God and is considered rebellion. And rebelling against God's direct command is compared to "sin of divination, and arrogance like the evil of idolatry" (1 Sam 15:23). Therefore, the Lord warned that there should not be anyone to be found among his chosen and his disciples who "practices divination or sorcery, interprets omens, engages in witchcraft" (Deut 18:10 NIV).

Nonetheless, the Lord encouraged Israel to trust in God and assured them that neither divination, witchcraft, nor sorcery will have any effect on those whom he has called to his name. There is no divination against Jacob and no evil omens against Israel works (Num 23:23). The Lord God has power and might to destroy witchcraft and dismantles its spells (Mic 5:12).

Therefore, we shall embrace the truth that our father invites us to become immersed in the divine story of his love and redemption of the world. As disciples, we are invited to discernment, the realization of our limitations, the need to depend on God's grace and the will for restoration. The call is to transform our perception and clarify that discipleship belongs to God and Israel is the disciple called to a continued partnership and cooperation with God. That, God alone is the caller of Israel and the teacher. Israel is the disciple beckoned to be a blessing and the light for the world (Isa 49:6). Until the promised time, the good news of redemption must be preached, the purpose of making disciples must continue so that the proclamation of the love of God to the whole world prevails.

Discipleship Model and Concept in the NT

> If you hold to my teaching, you are truly my disciples.
> Then you will know the truth, and the truth will set you
> free. (John 8:31 NIV)

This bold statement of Jesus grounds the whole concept and model of discipleship in the New Testament. And we can state that the term and concept of discipleship is portrayed vividly and becomes more familiar in the New Testament than it was in the Old Testament.

The term μαθητής (*mathétés* in Greek)[9] meaning "disciple" is the most used term in the NT. In fact, the followers of Jesus Christ were referred to as disciples more than they were called Christians. Statistically, they are called Christians three times only, but are disciples 250 times plus in the New Testament.[10] They are first called Christians in Antioch when they fled Jerusalem due to the eruption of persecution (Acts 11:26). The second place we see the word "Christian" was when King Agrippa wanted to silence Paul, claiming that Paul will not be able to persuade him to be a "Christian" in such a short period of time (Acts 26:28). Lastly, Peter used the word "Christians" when he tried to distinguish those who suffer for their own wrongdoing and those suffering as Christians for Christ (1 Pet 4:16).

Therefore, it must be true to say, as in the words of Dallas Willard, that "the New Testament is a book about disciples, by disciples, and for disciples of Jesus Christ."[11] We can agree with this claim. This is because even if discipleship was known during Jesus' time as it was descended from the OT, and the Jewish rabbis branded it, Jesus brought a new meaning to the concept and model of discipleship. He himself used the term (John 8:31) and people have associated his close circle of followers as disciples (Matt 15:2).

"Both words (*Christian and disciple*), imply a relationship with Jesus, although perhaps disciple is the stronger of the two because it inevitably implies the relationship of pupil to teacher. During his three years of public ministry the Twelve were disciples before they were apostles, and as disciples they were under the instruction of their teacher and Lord."[12]

As stated elsewhere in this project, discipleship starts with the call, the following, and the sending (Matt 4:18–22). In this regard, one cannot claim to be a disciple of Jesus before they are instructed and understand the meaning and purpose of the call and then sent as an apostle to witness the message of redemption (Mark 9:30–41).

9. "Mathétés."

10. McKenzie, *Dictionary of the Bible*, 199.

11. Willard, *Great Omission*, 202.

12. Stott, *Radical Disciple*, 14.

This happens in our faith journey. We are convicted, believe in Jesus Christ, then we are catechized and baptized. Our spiritual formation is our discipleship process and continual effort to know God and to understand the doctrine and the theology of his redemptive work through Christ. Then we develop a personal relationship or become friends with Jesus. Finally, we feel empowered at the right time to witness to others (Acts 1:6–8).

We then live our lives as apostles, people who are sent to proclaim the good news of salvation. Jesus needs his followers to be Christians as they receive him as their Lord and Savior; then disciples as they surrender to his authority and adhere to the instructions; lastly, they become apostles as they are sent into the world as witnesses to make disciples (John 8:31). A disciple is a person who heeds and adheres to the instructions and maintains a personal relationship with the teacher. *To be a disciple is to commit to understanding the purpose and taking the mind of the caller* (1 Cor 2:16). A disciple strives to implement and accomplish the objective of the leader.

We learn that as they commit to transmit their doctrine, the Jewish rabbis or the teachers of the law required their students to be exactly like themselves. They would expect their students to attain their personal dignity, do as exactly as they did, expect them to become rabbis under their respective instructions. Even if there are elements of similarities, Jesus took the discipleship practice to a different level: friendship, self-sacrifice, and partnership. He "demanded a more complete personal surrender to Himself than did the rabbis. His disciple must be willing to abandon father and mother, son and daughter, and to take up his cross and lose his life in the following of Jesus (Matthew 10:37ff; Lk 14:26ff)."[13]

In the New Testament discipleship model, we are called to practice Jesus' words and ways and commit to transmitting his doctrine (*teaching about the person and attributes of God*) and theology (*God's purpose and plan*) to others. This suggests that our response to our call is grounded in and with our identities. In our practice as trainees or disciples, we are enabled to navigate ways

---

13. McKenzie, *Dictionary of the Bible*, 200.

to communicate and understand God's redemptive purpose and resources invested in us through the power of Jesus.

In the efforts to enhance the discipleship model, the New Testament depicts three concentric types of disciples:

1. The nucleus circle—the Twelve (John 21:15)

2. The wider sphere—the Seventy-Two (Luke 10:1–23)

3. The broader circle—the multitude (Matt 4:25; Mark 3:20; Luke 12:1; John 6:2; Acts 5:14)

However, one must know that even if responsibility is given to disciples who fall into all the above circles it varies in terms of ministry and gifts. But in terms of the call for personal submission and adherence that is required by the Lord, disciples, irrespective of category or types, are called for one purpose—proclamation of God's redemptive work through Christ (1 Pet 2:9; Eph 1:4–11). The same requirements and responsibility—self-sacrifice and surrendering to Jesus' authority—are expected of disciples in all categories (Matt 10:43–45; Luke 14:26), and the same destiny awaits them all—the kingdom and life eternity with God (Rev 19:6; Matt 7:21).

If we understand the mind of Jesus, we could say that the Twelve represent ministers of the word and sacrament (pastors), missionaries, etc. The wider loop, which consists of the Seventy-Two, signifies the ministry of lay leaders (elders, deacons, evangelists, teachers, choirs, outreach preachers, etc.). Then the multitude can be applied to the larger assembly of God. Jesus applied such a model to help influence his followers, but for one goal. As the New Testament writers have hinted, when Jesus would sit to teach his disciples, the Twelve are first in the circle, then the Seventy-Two and the multitude. So, he wanted to maintain the leadership and the flow of the information for the greater goal.

Nonetheless, the call and the requirement for discipleship remains the same. We are chosen, treasures of God, priests for the new nation, and set apart as God's devoted ones. God has adopted us through and united us in Christ Jesus in order that we would "broadcast his glorious wonders *throughout the world*" (1 Pet 2:9 TPT).

This entails the whole spectrum of the discipleship model and purpose. There is no special unit, nor a status when it comes to the responsibility and reward for the ministry (Matt 18:1–5). Jesus prayed for all and is still offering prayers for us (John 17:6–26). Christ has called us to demonstrate our new birth in him and to live like a shining light on a hillside. As a light on a hillside is visible to all and as salt improves the taste of many foods, so should the example of our lives as Christians draw people to Christ. We cannot hide our faith from others if we truly live by the teachings of Christ. And when we live out our faith as Jesus demands of us, we are then giving God the glory and praise he deserves, as Jesus has said.

Regarding the model, Jesus' discipleship process differs from that of the OT and of the scribes or rabbis. First, Jesus' discipleship model is aimed more toward friendship than a master or disciple-teacher relationship (John 15:15). While remembering his instructions and honoring the relationship is important, Jesus needed his disciples to claim a personal relationship with him. He disclosed his mind and imparted his strength to his disciples in a way which an earthly master would not treat a servant (Matt 13:11; Eph 1:9).

Second, Jesus requires disciples to remain in him and abide in his teachings. Whoever determines and continues to *remain* or *abide*, μείνητε (*meinete*), from the verb μένω (*menou*),[14] is a true disciple of Jesus Christ (John 8:32). This means that as disciples, we are called to demonstrate an unyielding will for learning and understanding the mind of God through his word—the Bible (2 Tim 3:16). Thirdly, unlike the rabbis of the first century, Jesus did not expect his disciples to memorize his teachings, nor to know his words by heart exactly as he taught them.[15] Rather, he promised to be present: the Holy Spirit will continue the teaching, remind us, and give what to say (John 14:26; Matt 10:19).

---

14. "Menó."

15. McKenzie, *Dictionary of the Bible*, 199–200.

In conclusion, Jesus' model of discipleship differs greatly from others because he himself knows God, came from him, and is one with him. We can say that the disciples are receiving fresh information sourcing right from God. He claimed and said, "Whatever I say is just what the Father has told me to say" (John 12:49–50; 16:28).

As disciples, we are given the task to proclaim the message of redemption and love of God sourcing directly from the throne of glory. Yes, our Lord "invites each of us to become immersed in the story of his Word, which includes great deeds, adventure, love, betrayal, sacrifice, miracles, and much more. . . . the scriptures give us a story in which we can meet God himself, come to know his infinite love for each of us, and respond to his invitation to enter into this epic tale."[16] Therefore, if we are his disciples as we proclaim, we should do his will and surrender to his authority, in that we are given the right to call him Lord and teacher (Luke 6:46). We should hold on to his teachings, know the truth; we are set free to liberate others from the chains of this world.

The Concept of Marriage and Divinities in the NT

1. Marriage, Divorce, and Polygamy

As we now know, discipleship is a call to transformation and to immerse ourselves in God's salvific story. It is a life that requires substantial change and mindfulness of Jesus' instructions in our faith journey. In discipleship we identify ourselves with Jesus and acquire a mature relationship. In this regard, the matters of marriage, divorce, and polygamy must be discussed when we talk about discipleship. We will not explore this topic in depth but will encourage the reader to see our discussion under the OT concept on this topic.

However, like the Old Testament, the New Testament opposed the idea of a divorce without substantial reason and polygamy, and maintained that marriage is a gift of God for the well-being of the

16. Gray and Cavins, *Walking with God*, 1–2.

family of faith. In the Epistles to the Ephesians, Paul exemplified the unity of the church with Jesus as a symbol of marriage. Paul claims that this union as such is Jesus' marriage to the church whose members he had called from the world as disciples to make known God's purpose (Eph 5:31–32). As C. S. Lewis has said, the Christian's concept of marriage is based on "Christ's words that a man and wife are to be regarded as a single organism—for that is what the words 'one flesh' would be in modern English. And the Christian believes that when He said this, He was not expressing a sentiment but stating a fact—just as one is stating a fact when one says that a lock and its key are one mechanism, or that a violin and a bow are one musical instrument."[17] One cannot function without the other but remains as a single entity with no effect. Marriage has an element of mystery that the disciples of Christ are encouraged to understand. The unity between the husband (male) and wife (female) is the tip of the iceberg. But the mystery of marriage rests with God and represents the inseparable trinitarian bond—the Father, the Son, and the Holy Spirit are One (Matt 28:19; John 10:30).

Therefore, the New Testament requires that everyone should honor marriage, not only a few or leaders of the church as some perceive Paul's instruction wrongly (1 Tim 3:1–12). In Christian marriage, the couple are combined not merely "on the sexual level, but totally combined" ontologically.[18] That marriage must be kept pure as we offer respect to God in the relationship. Anything we do outside of marriage is rejecting God's plan for us and God does not condone such disobedience (Heb 13:4).

The life of a disciple is a life of determination and decision-making. *We live by putting our own life aside and being clothed with the life of Christ and walking in the light of the demands of God.* This includes how we maintain our marriages and aspire to say "no" to "ungodliness and worldly passions, and to live self-controlled, upright, and godly lives in this present age" (Titus 2:12–14 NIV).

17. Lewis, *Mere Christianity*, 81.

18. Lewis, *Mere Christianity*, 81.

2. *Divinities, Sorcery, and Witchcraft*

> There may be so-called gods both in heaven and on earth, and some people actually worship many gods and many lords. But for us,
>
> There is one
>
> God, the Father,
> by whom all things were created,
> and for whom we live.
> And there is one Lord, Jesus Christ,
> through whom all things were created,
> and through whom we live. (1 Cor 8:5–7 NLT)

This passage summarizes the New Testament position on the existence of other gods, spirits, and demons. Yet, the NT maintains that such subjects are simply contesting forces originating from Satan, the force of the darkness that controlled the atmosphere (Eph 2:2). That the disciples of Christ must not fear nor revere them because there is only one almighty God, whom even the demons believe and tremble in terror of his name (Jas 2:19).

In specific terms, disciples are called to treat such understandings as influences and are called for the need to drive them out and to heal the soul that is infested by such influences so that the individual may come to the realization of the true God and praise him as the Lord. The NT perceives such beliefs as hindrances that hold people back from following God. We read about Elymas the deceiver and fraudulent (Acts 13:8); Simon, the manipulator (Acts 8:9–25); the fortune teller house girl (Acts 16:16–21); the violent tomb dwellers of Gadarenes (Matt 8:28–34); the goddess Artemis (Acts 19:23–41); etc., only to list a few.

As we can read from the above examples, these spirits try to keep people from believing, place doubts in individuals, and disguise themselves in deception to prevent us from doing what is good for the Lord (2 Cor 11:14). Long before Christ was revealed, we lived like the people of Athens, who had been worshiping God but with a wrong representation (Acts 17:22–23). Now like Paul, we are called to make known the God whom people worship in a different way. We are encouraged to put on the full armor of God (Eph 6:10–17), and empowered to proclaim the good news, cast out demons, and heal the suffering souls as everyone needs deliverance for Christ (Mark 16:18–20).

Christ Jesus has invested the power in us to not "give the devil a foothold" but make converts (Eph 4:27 NIV). The overall objective of discipleship "is to make converts, people who believe the gospel, repent of their former way of life, a bonfire of the vanities, and face a new direction—Christward."[19] A convert is one who repents of the past, turns around, and faces the future with faith in Jesus. Therefore, *we must claim all territories, defeat the sorcerers, witches, etc. for Christ, and shame the devil* (Jas 4:7).

Early Church Discipleship Approaches

It all began in the upper room where the disciples had gathered after returning from Mount of Olives in Bethany where Jesus ascended to heaven. At this moment, the disciples were not only facing an identity issue, but also a direction now that Jesus existed no longer in his physical persona. The last thing they could do was to worship him while Jesus floated from the ground into the sky and a cloud swallowed him up. They came back to Jerusalem with competing thoughts about the "Galileans" who stared at the sky (Luke 24:50–53) and the eschatological anticipation as the angels had promised (Acts 1:11). We can assume that the disciples were recalling Jesus's words: remember everything I had told you, because they shall keep you from stumbling (John 16:1–4).

The purpose of discipleship is *to lay a faithful foundation so that a believer understands God and his divine redemptive purpose.* It is to establish our cooperation and claim personal relationship with Christ Jesus. Discipleship is being in motion yet knowing the real Jesus. This was a remarkable moment in the life of the disciples' post-Jesus earthly life. It was indeed the fullness

---

19. Vanhoozer, *Faith Speaking Understanding*, xxiv.

of time and God had prepared for this moment and in all the historical circumstances.[20]

The disciples remained in constant prayer after returning from the Mount of Olives seeking the face of the Lord for directions (Acts 1:12–14). Surely, Pentecost was the answer and the fulfillment of the promise of empowerment (Acts 1:8). And then the great sermon of Peter had gained three thousand converts and the number kept adding up. The disciples knew that conversion must be guided by elements of Christian formation to make faithful disciples. Therefore, all believers, without exception, devoted themselves to the teachings, to fellowship, to sharing generosities, to prayer, and to praising God in worship (Acts 2:42–47).

This discipleship model continued throughout the early church. After so much experience in missionary work, Paul sought to change his strategic method to the discipleship approach of teaching. While in Ephesus, he rented a lecture hall of Tyrannus and conducted daily teachings and discussions for two years. The result was astonishing, "everyone living in the province of Asia, Jews and Gentiles," heard the word of the Lord (Acts 19:8–10 NIV). He continued with this approach even while he was in the Roman prison cell for two years (Acts 28:23–31). Even during his missionary years, Paul tended to engage in a teacher-disciple approach and his method worked (Acts 16:13–15; 18:27; 19:1–7; etc.).

As Justo L. Gonzalez stated, Paul's success and contribution in "shaping the early Christianity was not so much in the actual founding of churches. Rather, it was in the epistles that he wrote in connection with that activity since those epistles eventually became part of Christian Scriptures and thus have had a decisive and continuing impact in the life and thought of the Christian church."[21] In this regard, we learn that the early church did not take the discipleship process and ministry lightly. Rather, catechumens (new converts) would commit to a three-year discipleship training before baptism. They would continue with basic theological instructions

20. Gonzalez, *Story of Christianity*, 7.

21. Gonzalez, *Story of Christianity*, 25. See Barclay, *Letter to the Romans*, 91.

to help them understand God, what God has done in Christ, and about Jesus and his redemption. Before baptism, they are required to answer question of basics of the Christian faith.[22] Baptism was considered as a dividing line in person's life, and like those entering Judaism, a person would be undressed, cut their nails and hair, and descend into the waters; when they emerged, it symbolized rising to new life like Jesus.[23] Yet, as William Barclay stated, symbolism become "real only when a [person] believed intensely in the life and death and resurrection of Jesus Christ."[24] Disciples make a conscious decision to live as disciples.

The early church understood that as we unite in Christ, we also grow in the grace and knowledge of the gospel and Jesus becomes our friend, like God to Abraham (Gen 18:16–18; 2 Pet 3:18). Who will not be bold to talk about a friend's best attributes? That is the mystery of discipleship (John 8:32; 16:1) and the church has kept this tradition, passed it on, and has enriched it over the years.

Ecclesiastical Endeavor to Enhance Discipleship

As stated above, discipleship remained as an important part of mission and evangelism in the life of the Christian church. The church strongly believes that discipleship helps believers identify themselves with Jesus, keeps them from stumbling, and provides a knowledge of God, where a believer is empowered to share the gospel of Christ. The longer you learn about Jesus, the more you aspire to serve and share him.

Therefore, the reformers placed great emphasis on teaching and learning to improve and advance the practice of discipleship. In their endeavor, history has recorded them as the giants of Christian education. In the medieval church, Reformation era, much emphasis was placed on church teachings as part of discipleship

---

22. Bradshaw, "Concerning Confessors."

23. Barclay, *Letter to the Romans*, 82–85.

24. Barclay, *Letters to the Philippians*, 140

training. As a result, the Bible became available for any regular believer who could read. In 1528, Martin Luther dedicated sermons to catechism, highlighting the fundamentals of Christian knowledge and the importance of learning. The more a person studied, the more learned they became.[25] These expositions would become small and large catechism materials for discipleship and faith formation instructions.

In Geneva, John Calvin was bold to introduce an article which was adopted by the city council. The article emphasized the importance of religious education and children being trained regularly in the fundamentals of the Christian faith.[26] As Herman J. Selderhuis demonstrated, Calvin strongly believed that "the church of God will never preserve itself without a Catechism, for it is like the seed to keep the good grain from dying out and causing it to multiply from age to age."[27]

As part of the development and aspiration to improve discipleship ministry, "interpretation, commentaries, and sermons on the Catechism are also documented."[28] Calvin insisted that the church be given the responsibility to teach faithful disciples of Christ. He claimed that teaching is the beginning of our salvation. That teaching enters in the "interior of the heart and shows its power in our life, indeed even transforms us into its nature."[29]

Discipleship has shaped Christian tradition and has contributed to Christian theology from medieval thoughts and idealistic views. We can even claim that the Reformation of the sixteenth century was part of the enhancement of the discipleship teachings. Reformers such as Luther, Calvin, and Zwingli, as well as different reformations in Europe and awakenings in America, have played a great role in this progress.[30] The result of Reformation would affect the world, even the world outside the church as

25. Dillenberger, *Martin Luther*, 208

26. Shillington, *History of Africa*, 207.

27. Shillington, *History of Africa*, 206.

28. Shillington, *History of Africa*, 213.

29. Calvin, *Institutes*, 683–84.

30. Mullin, *World History of Christianity*, 171.

it affected common people. Through these movements, Christian missions to other nations and the development of theology in Christianity, as well as the modern world, came into existence. To establish Christianity in the New World with reasoning, many universities were built through Europe and America.[31] Enlightenment, industrialization, and modern civilization evolved. In Thomas Münzer's words, the Reformation made "people go free and God alone will be their Lord."[32]

Through mission organizations, missionaries flooded into the world proclaiming the good news all around the continents. They enlightened the understandings of the natives about God to avoid myths of a multiplicity of gods and avoid the fear of spirits.[33] To step up their discipleship processes, missionaries translated the Bible into native languages for same purpose.[34] They offered literacy programs teaching the natives to learn and read. As it was said, "If there was one word that epitomized the nineteenth-century imagination, it would be 'progress.'"[35]

The great endeavor and the resource development by church leaders in the early, medieval, Reformation, and missionary eras should hearten us; and we must build on their work rather than diminishing the importance of discipleship. Discipleship does not end with the profession of faith or receiving baptism but includes continuing to learn how to live out Christ's will in our life and being transformed into his likeness by the renewing of our minds (Rom 12:2; Gal 2:20).

31. Mullin, *World History of Christianity*, 164–74.

32. Lindberg, *European Reformation*, 130.

33. Achebe, *Things Fall Apart*, 144–47.

34. Hoekstra, *Honey, We're Going*, 104–22.

35. Mullin, *World History of Christianity*, 187.

CHAPTER 3

The Role of Culture and Tradition in Discipleship Approaches

A Brief Historical Background of the Anyuwaa People

THIS CHAPTER INTRODUCES, PRELIMINARILY, the origin, social system, economic system, political system, traditions, and religious practices of the Anyuwaa people and how they affect discipleship ministry and approaches in the church of Christ. The reader will find this chapter crucial as it solidifies the project's purpose. It provides facts for the background and plays a significant role in presenting genuine information for the achievement of the intended outcome of the project. This is because the scope of history, tradition, and cultural rites are crucial elements that *affect the discipleship practices and ministry* of the Anyuwaa church and our lives as followers of Christ.

Etymology

The name Anyuwaa is derived from the word *Nyuwak* meaning "sharing," and Anyuwaa means "I share" or "of sharing." However, due to mispronunciation of the word by the Ethiopian governors sent by emperors from the North and Central Ethiopia to govern the Gambella region in the years past, they misspelled the word, changing it from "the Anyuwaa" to "Anuak." Gambella became part of Ethiopia by the landmark agreement of May 15, 1902, between the Anglo-Egyptian Sudan under the British rule and Emperor Menelik II.[1] This historical event marked the inclusion of the Gambella region into the Ethiopian territory and brought the rise of Gambella with the port of Itang serving as a trade hub between Sudan and Ethiopia. The Opëno or Baro river was used as the trade route, and 10 percent of the annual exports were secured through Gambella-Sudan trade where the Ethiopians shipped coffee and the British brought cotton and salt in exchange.[2]

Nevertheless, those governors who were appointed periodically, were Amharic speakers who did not know the Anyuwaa language, and the Anyuwaa did not speak Amharic at the time. A few might have spoken the Oromo language of their close neighbors to the east. And oral tradition indicated that the governors used interpreters of Oromo speakers to communicate with the Anyuwaa people. The Amharic language has a tendency to add suffixes etymologically, most certainly when it comes to possessive forms. For example, while the ethnicity is Amhara, the language is *Amharinya*; "English" becomes *Englizenya*; and "Arabic" *Arabenya*; etc. These etymological orders engender changes in both the sound of the words and the words they modify. These new residents did not adhere to the use of the terms and names of the inhabitants, including names of the rivers, hills, lakes, etc. in the Anyuwaa Gambella region.

Therefore, the Anyuwaa language and the ethnic name were not spared from such mistakes that have passed through generations and international recognition of the names. And the world has adapted to this misleading etymology. Consequently, ethnologists and anthropologists, historians, and missionaries[3] have adopted similar misspellings in their written works, and many have

1. Zewde, "'Twixt Sirdar and Emperor."
2. Zewde, "'Twixt Sirdar and Emperor."
3. McClure, *Red-Headed*, 57.

spelled the term differently: Anuak, Anywaa,[4] and others such as Agnwak,[5] Anyuak, Anyuwaa, etc.

While the world knows the ethnic group by the name "Anuak," the indigenous call themselves the Anyuwaa (singular) and Jø-Anyuwaa or Anyuwaee (plural), meaning the Anyuwaa people, and the language is Dha-Anyuwaa (the Anyuwaa language). Currently, Jø Anyuwaa are found both in Ethiopia and Southern Sudan, and the same language is spoken rightly by the Anyuwaa in both countries.

The Origin of the Anyuwaa People

Anthropological Findings

The Anyuwaa tribe is part of the larger Luo ethnic community of East Africa. The Luo people are scattered in many countries in East Africa due to migration in centuries past. The Anyuwaa claim to have preserved the Luo cultural heritage due to their minimal exposure to outside influences, their resistance to intrusions, and avoidance of interethnic marital relationships with the neighboring ethnic communities in their current locations.[6] Those in Ethiopia are ethnically, culturally, linguistically, historically, and religiously different from other Ethiopian ethnic groups.

Ethnologists and anthropologists have categorized the Anyuwaa people into the Nilotes ethnic groups who speak Nilotic languages of Nilo-Saharan Africa. Even if the Nilotes have common features of language, and culture, the Anyuwaa are classified as part of the northern Luo group with whom they have close linguistic and cultural distinctive features. They are close relatives to the Shilluk, the Acholi and Päri (or Jø Punyuaa, as the Anyuwaa called them) of South Sudan, the Acholi of Uganda, and the Luo of Kenya.[7]

4. Kurimoto, "Natives and Outsiders," 3.

5. Perner, *Sphere of Spirituality*, 24.

6. Zewde, "'Twixt Sirdar and Emperor," 79–93.

7. Perner, *Sphere of Spirituality*, 23.

Regarding their historical origin, no one has pinpointed convincingly the origin of the Anyuwaa people because the Luo community was so widespread throughout East Africa. It was believed that the Anyuwaa must have moved to their current location either from the land of the Nilotes near the town of Rumbek in South Sudan or perhaps from the southeast region near Lake Rudolph in Kenya during the period of high migration between the sixteenth and the nineteenth centuries. And many believe that the preceding location has more convincing evidence than the latter, because the Päri or Jø Punyuaa in the Southern Sudan are believed to be part of the larger Luo lineage who were left behind during migration.[8] Yet, a few traced the Anyuwaa residences to their current country back from 1450 BC[9] or the early ADs.[10]

Like their relatives—the Shilluk, Acholi, and Luo of Kenya— the Anyuwaa are "a riverain people living along"[11] the lakes and rivers of Opëënö, Gilø, Akööbö, Alwørø, Cïiru, Oböth, Thatha, etc. and their tributaries both in Pochalla, South Sudan, and the western region of Ethiopia. The Anyuwaa have been pushed eastward by the Murle and mainly the Nuer tribe which resulted in absorbing many Anyuwaa areas on Sobat and Opëënö River to the west.[12] Since the downfall of the Dergue regime of Mengistu Hailemariam in 1991, many villages on the Opëënö riverbank have once again been occupied by the Nuer ethnic tribes driving out the Anyuwaa people.[13] In addition, the sum of the twenty-one years of the Sudan civil war and the current tribal war of December, 2023 between the Dinka and the Nuer has affected the Anyuwaa directly. Nuer absorbed more land and villages due

8. Perner, *Sphere of Spirituality*, 23.

9. Shillington, *History of Africa*, 116–20.

10. Kirwan, "Ethiopian-Sudanese Frontier."

11. Evans-Pritchard, *Political System*, 7–9; see also Perner, *Sphere of Spirituality*, 23–25.

12. Evans-Pritchard, *Political System*, 6–7.

13. Villages include Cïrö, Aköbö-Tiergool, Aduu-Jwøki, Inyoon, Pinyngiew, Pinythø, Ideni, Caam, Pinykew, Iudo, Okoorgääla, Pojöö, Imedhø, Pinymøngø, Potøk, Ilia-Kiirageeta, Punyuaa, Itiel, Adïima, Pokedi, Owaalø and recently Pino.

to the unsecured border that has resulted in the influx of count-less Nuer into the Gambella region. While the Anyuwaa were the majority in the region out of a population of 181,860, according to the 1994 census, now the Anyuwaa of Gambella account for only 21.16 percent of 307,096, according to the 2007 Ethiopian Census.[14]

Besides the Nuers' aggression, the Anyuwaa have been resist-ing any occupation by the two governments of Ethiopia and Sudan before and since the establishment of the countries and border landmarks. There were incidents of invasions at Akobo in Sudan and the Gambella area where the two governments squeezed the Anyuwaa from both sides like a meat patty in a sandwich.[15] Their fertile land, rich wildlife, fishery, and minerals have been their assets to protect from unlawful harvest by those they consider outsiders. The current incident occurred on December 13, 2003, where the Ethiopian Army targeted the Anyuwaa and massacred their men.[16] As a result, many Anyuwaa migrated and now live in South Sudan, Uganda, and Kenya Refugee camps. However, it is believed that the Ethiopian and Sudan governments have suc-ceeded in "destroying practically all traditional Anyuwaa values" since Gambella was added into Ethiopian territory.[17]

Oral Traditions

The Anyuwaa, like many African tribes, maintain their informa-tion and historical facts orally, and such information is passed on in the form of folktales (*waac*) or riddles (*leere*) and demon-strated through performances and objects. Due to the limitation of my work, I will briefly explain the oral tradition and related information, but I encourage the reader to review materials re-lated to this topic.

14. Office of Population and Housing Census Commission, *1994 Popula-tion and Housing Census*, 5–6.

15. Zewde, "'Twixt Sirdar and Emperor."

16. "Ethiopia: Crimes Against Humanity."

17. Perner, *Sphere of Spirituality*, 23.

Regarding human origin, the Anyuwaa traced their origin from the creation story of humanity. Though they have different versions in their oral tradition, the Anyuwaa believed that after God caused everything else to be born, God lastly delivered twin creatures. While some oral versions give the names of the twins as Cwääy (male) and Määrö (female) or Opiew (male) and Acään (female), other traditions are told with no mention of names but only *gïr Gwök*, meaning a thing that belongs to the dog. These creatures looked ugly in God's sight and God said, "Why did my belly bring forth these alien creatures?" Then God caused God's womb to dry up and bear no more creatures like these new beings.

God decided to kill the two creatures. However, a dog, who was God's assistant at the time, sneaked the Opiew and Acään to an unknown location. When God asked the dog about the whereabouts of the creatures, the dog simply lay down, wagging his tail to show that he did not know. The dog got slimmer from starvation as the dog kept passing the food to his pets. When God would give food to the dog, the dog would take the portion to Opiew and Acään until the twins grew bigger, and he could not hide them anymore. Now when God finally saw humans (Opiew and Acään), he found them to be good looking creatures. "You don't need to hide them; they will stay here at home and I myself will take care of them," said God to the dog.

At one time when God created tools and wanted to divide them among his creatures for use, God preferred to introduce them to Buffalo first and give him the best tools. This is because Buffalo was God's friend at the time. However, while God was telling Buffalo to be first in line in the early morning when he gave out gifts of tools, the dog pretended to be sleeping but was listening to the whole conversation. This is because God said, "gïr Gwök waange riek," meaning the one that belongs to the dog is wise—when talking about humans.

The dog came and related all he had heard between God and Buffalo to humans and advised them to leave early in the morning before the rooster crowed to be first in the line. Mornings in Anyuwaa are determined based on when a rooster crows in the morning.

When the rooster crows is the time people wake up for a journey, for farming, hunting, etc. Birds sing later in the morning, but the rooster crows at around 4:30 a.m. or 5:00 a.m. When a rooster crows at a wrong time, the Anyuwaa would say, "*Gwenø gwäädö*," meaning the roster is foretelling something devastating.

Humans heeded the advice of the dog and went to God when God was inside the storeroom arranging the tools. Early in the morning, God heard feet outside the storeroom and when he had asked who that might be, the human said, "Buffalo." Then God threw out spears, hoes, etc. and the humans took the best tools God had made. Unfortunately, Buffalo woke up late and came at last when the good tools had already been dispensed. God said, "I do not have anything left except for these big horns, here just take them and carry them on your head." The buffalo took them and still has big horns, even today.

While human beings lived together with the rest of the creations of God, a division occurred because of a great famine that struck the land. Sin increased as many tried to steal and do irresponsible things. *God transcended above the sky and human beings left God's home, "Po Jwøk,"* and migrated to various locations in the world along with many animals. The Anyuwaa, in the leadership of their leader Cwääy[18] were the first clans to depart the area.[19] This relates and resembles the story of the fall in the Genesis account.

Yet, other oral traditions hold that part of the Anyuwaa lineage did not have any origin but emerged from the river and therefore the Anyuwaa are always found living on riverbanks or on lakes, including the Shilluk and Luo, their close relatives. To this day, the Anyuwaa claim that they are the firstborn of God or have a special space with God, saying, "Anyuwaa nyilewiinh Jwøk," meaning "the Anyuwaa are God's favorites." Regarding their migration to their current location, the Anyuwaa traced their origin from deep in South Sudan and as far as Egypt. Many claim that the Anyuwaa were inhabitants of Khartoum in centuries past and that the name itself is derived from the Anyuwaa

18. Shillington, *History of Africa*, 119.
19. Wall, "Anuak Politics, Ecology."

language *kartum*, meaning "a fishing place," since Khartoum lies on the Nile River.[20] Also, the former South Sudan leader Dr. John Gerang de Mabior once said that even before Khartoum the Anyuwaa had lived in Egypt and worshiped their god Anuk, who held the key to gates of the waters of the Nile River.[21]

Sociological and Cultural Reflections

The Anyuwaa are defined and reflected by their own name of sharing, *Nyuwak*. It is their identity and an indispensable motto. Their social life and fabric are interwoven around their claim of their common life, and they are proud of this identity. The Anyuwaa share many things if not everything.

This ethnic group has distinct *social systems and structural dynamics* unlike their surrounding neighbors of Nuer, Murle, and Majang. Surrounding their social life and structure, the Anyuwaa value *Wïmaac*. Wimaac is a men-only space, usually situated at the edge of a village. In a village of the Anyuwaa you will find three or more *Wïth-mäc (pl)*. Two, three, or four household relatives form a *Wïmaac*. Here, key issues of family are discussed, planned for, solved, or executed. Issues of dowry, weddings, instructions, and vengeance of a relative's blood are discussed. However, matters regarding war, mass hunting, and restitution for the blood of someone who was killed by a villager without intent are discussed in the court of the headman, or the chief of the village.

In this societal structure, a male is the head of the household, followed by the woman, older children, etc. At *Wimaac* the heads of the households, meaning males, dine together in one setting; women also eat together, and children share their meals together as well. A boy stays within the women's court until he turns twelve or at a mature stage where he can go fishing, hunting, etc. Until he is capable enough to do men's work, a boy stays with women. Widows, orphans, and elders are taken care of by

20. Shillington, *History of Africa*, 119.
21. Askou100, "Dr Garang's."

relatives as well as by villagers at large. The Anyuwaa do not want anyone left to starvation or in a state of material need. While women are responsible for childcare, food, and all housework, men are solely responsible for the work outside the house. Even if there are a few exceptions, a man farms, hunts, and in general, he provides for the needs of the household. He spends the day at *Wïmaac* and only comes to his home for sleep, if he is sick, or needs to do something around the house, including building a hut or maintaining the fence. Home belongs to the woman, as they say in Dha-Anyuwaa, "paac a po dhaagø."

Regarding ordinances, the Anyuwaa maintain that a person is who he/she is because community exists in their cultural setting. This moral value shapes the moral ethics of every child from birth throughout one's entire life. Necessarily, everyone is responsible for the best of the community. Whenever someone fails to meet the standard of this role, such a person will be condemned as a failure. He or she will be considered *patha-dhaannhø*, literally, "not a human," because in Anyuwaa to be a human is to be whole in essence and has a deep meaning. The Anyuwaa believe that there are beings that may appear in a physical or spiritual form but are hostile and cause chaos and destruction for human beings. Thus, an Anyuwaa must show clearly that he or she is well and truly human—such fully human identity must be shown by love, sharing, hard work, and care for the poor in the community.[22] As such, the Anyuwaa life is structured around age group and gender as well as a strong legal system. People of each group do things together and share in a communal life as their custom. Therefore, everyone heeds the instructions of, obeys, and honors the elders and respects guests. Unlike the Nuers and Murle, their close neighbors, economic influence does not have any merit in the Anyuwaa society.

They are riverain people who inhabited fertile lands on the riverbanks mentioned above. Their economy is based on fishery, farming, hunting, gathering, and herding cattle. The Anyuwaa living downstream of Opëënö, those in Jöör, Cïrö, Adööngö, raise cattle. Only a pocket of the Anyuwaa in the northeast and center

22. Perner, *Human Territory*, 25.

of Anyuwaa country predominantly live on farming, hunting, and gathering of roots and leaves. As modernization changed the enterprise, many Anyuwaa in Gambella are government employees and are living on earned wages, but only a few are business owners. Above all, the Anyuwaa people "are excellent farmers and can feed themselves and others quite well; they are generally healthy-looking people, in spite of frequent floods and droughts which force them to live upon grass or roots for months or to seek help from relatives living in less affected areas of the country."[23]

The Anyuwaa Traditional Leadership and Political System

As we aim to develop a practical discipleship model that fosters spiritual maturity in the Anyuwaa church, the issue compels us to explore leadership and political systems as it inevitably affects the leadership and discipleship model of the Anyuwaa church. The Anyuwaa people have two types of leadership and political systems, which for the sake of this project we will briefly discuss here. Long before the outsiders set foot on the Anyuwaa land, the Anyuwaa people had already established a functional leadership style and two leadership systems called *kwär*, meaning "chiefship," led by a *Kwäärö* (a "chief"), and *Nyec* ("kingship"), headed by a *Nyeya* (a "king"). While the previous functions in a democratic system, the latter is monarchical. When it comes to their difference, while the chief (*Kwäärö*) can be deposed and leave the throne, a king (*Nyeya*) must be killed to be replaced. This resonates with Jesus' claim regarding his purpose as a King to the world (John 18:37)

Under chiefship, *Kwäärö*, or the chief, is the political headmaster of the village. Each village is independent, has its own chief or a representative of a chief who acts as an executive steward of the affairs of such an autonomous village.[24] In their political system, the chief serves as the executive branch of his chiefdom.

23. Perner, *Sphere of Spirituality*, 23.
24. Evans-Pritchard, *Political System*, 9.

While the chief cannot be voted in and out, he can be deposed and replaced by a brother, a cousin, or a member of his close lineage with the help of their allies. A chief can be deposed for three main reasons: *inability to execute matters of the village effectively (judiciary), failing to provide for the village (economy), or failing to protect the well-being of his people (security). However, a chief is rarely assassinated.* A deposed chief must leave the village entirely and go to his or her uncle's village where his mother came from. Rarely a deposed chief can be reinstated if his/her staunch supporters quell the rebellion of the other group.

While chiefship was the oldest leadership system in the Anyuwaa society started from their founding father, Cwääy, or "Chwezi,"[25] kingship is an emerging leadership style and was a result of a mysterious man called Ocwudhö, which means "a person of a stump." The issue of fair judgment was critical at that time. The myth stated that, on one occasion while the boys were fishing in a river, they caught a catfish. Since they were fishing by hand, one of the boys caught the fish by the tail and the other by the head. An argument and quarrel broke out between the two, each claiming the ownership of the fish. Suddenly, a stranger appeared from the river. The women had spotted this man a few times sitting on a stump by the riverside whenever they would go fetch water. Yet, the man would quickly disappear into the water to avoid contact with them.

However, after asking the boys what they were arguing about, he instructed the boy who had held the fish by its head to leave the fish for the other who had the tail. Then the fish slipped away because you cannot hold the fish by its tail. The next day when the boys returned for fishing, they caught a fish in a comparable way. This time, the man instructed the boy who held the fish by its tail to release his hand from the fish. Rightly, the fish did not slip away. "From now on," he said, "when two people catch a fish one holds the tail and the other the head, the person holding the tail must leave the fish to the ones holding it by its head, it does belong to that person."

25. Shillington, *History of Africa*, 119.

This was a well-executed judgment for the ancient Anyuwaa society. The boys went home rejoicing, and the news went around the village and the chief received it as well. The chief instructed his men to bring home the stranger who was wise in his judgment. They called him Ocwudhö because he resided on the stump from a floating log. However, the man would not talk whenever he was asked and did not eat nor drink when he was provided with food. They placed him in his own hut and the chief asked his daughter to care for the wise man. The daughter first took water and food and placed it at the door and left without saying a word to him. Ocwudhö began to eat, drink, and he developed a relationship with the girl. Unfortunately, the princess conceived and was pregnant with a baby from the wise man. Then Ocwudhö disappeared to the river in fear that the chief might harm him. Ocwudhö did not return but was a responsible person. In his departure, he left behind special bead for dowry. When the princess gave birth to a boy, they named him Giillø, meaning a "solid bump, or a stomach swelling" because the princess was not aware of the pregnancy and had been telling her friends she might have a bump in her belly.

Time passed, and famine struck the land. Cwääy, the chief, had asked his only son to find food from a far distant of the Anyuwaa land. Upon his return, the boy did not want to share the food with the villagers nor with his father. The father asked his guards to go bind and bring the boy to his court. However, the prince was killed in the operation because the guard misunderstood the instructions. While the chief meant *kälu,* which means "bring him," the guard thought the chief said *këëllu,* meaning "hit him with spear."

The chief was furious and acted wildly. Rather than acting against the guard, the chief enacted a harsh law, saying from this time on, human for human, leg for leg, eye for eye, tooth for tooth, and hand for hand, as in the ancient Israel's code of law (Exod 21:23–25; Lev 24:20; Deut 19:21). He restricted the law from any opinion. And examination of the condition was prohibited.

Currently his grandson was growing and always sitting quietly by his grandparent's side when executing judgments. The boy was full of wisdom and began to defuse disputes between his peers during their play time outside the court of the chief. He began giving advice to his grandfather little by little, and his judgments were satisfactory to the community. People began seeking his service to resolve disputes rather than going to the chief. The chief did not interpret this situation as rebellion, and the boy who has no father is always his son. Since he lost his only son, the chief decided to leave the throne and be succeeded by Giillø who became the first king and brought kingship to the Anyuwaa leadership and political system.

When it comes to their difference, while the chief (*Kwäärö*) can be deposed and leave the throne, a king (*Nyeya*) must be killed to be replaced. Even if it was rarely practiced, both political systems are gender inclusive. A daughter can replace her father after his death. Similarly, both play political roles and lead their villages in time of famine and war. They rally their men to defend the village and work hard to avoid starvation. They provide wealth to the poor and unmarried individuals for dowry so that they can secure families for the village.

While they do not have religious power as such tasks are given to a different lineage in the village, kings and chiefs are believed to have divine elements. When they die, they are buried in a special place called *dwöl*, an open grave made from a hut covered with mud. Yet, the Anyuwaa hold that kings and chiefs do not die, but only "return," as they would say in Dha-Anyuwaa "adøø naam" meaning he or she has returned to the river. Water, *Pïï* in Anyuwaa, is considered as a symbol of existence and of life. As Conradin Perner observed, water "appears to be the element of transition between the spiritual and the material, carrier of the stream of eternal life, the transcendence and the consciousness of the material and the fecundity of earthly existence."[26] This concept of returning to waters originated from the ancient belief that the Anouk god has the key to the Nile River. This is the reason the Anyuwaa seek to reside on the stream of waters then during migrations and now in their current locations.

26. Perner, *Human Territory*, 30.

As water covers many aspects in Christian belief, water has special place in the Anyuwaa social life and belief system. Water flows through rivers, falls from skies, but is potent to carry things, and retain its existence in lakes, pools, and ponds—it is a living element. "Pïï mo rïïëngö beeye Pïï mo kwøw," meaning running or flowing water is a living water, they say. This confirms the concept of baptism to new life through waters (John 3:5). In the ancient church, the catechists were made to pass through the waters and emerged as new human beings with renewed attitude, continuing to learn, and remain disciples in the Christian church.

The Anyuwaa Traditional Religion

When Jesus asked his disciples, "Who do people say I am?" the disciples' answers reflected their understanding from their Jewish religious knowledge, saying, "John the Baptist," "Elijah," and "one of the prophets." Peter's application of Jewish religious knowledge revealed the truth of who Jesus is: "*You are the Christ*" (Mark 8:28, 29). This is clearly true that to better understand the Christian faith, we cannot ignore our previous religious under-standings and experiences, as they play significant role in our new religious faith. As Diane B. Stinton said, "That's why some of us go back into African traditional religion and African culture, to see what images, what symbols, are there, which will help us to understand who Jesus is."[27]

As one of the African traditional religions, the Anyuwaa reli-gious practices contain rich elements that *can be applied and used in our discipleship process, church ministry, and faith formation.* Diane Stinton is right, in that for the Anyuwaa church to remain faithful in the mission of the church, we must not ignore but incorporate such beliefs, rites, and images of the Anyuwaa tradition into our church practices and discipleship process and ministry.

The Anyuwaa people have beliefs, spirituality, and cus-toms they practice expressing the existence of the divine and its

27. Stinton, *Jesus of Africa*, 138.

relationship to the physical world. Jø Anyuwaa are religious, and their worldview includes strong belief in spiritual matters. They have distinct views regarding spiritual realms and physical matters. Their customary practices exhibit the essence of life in its present state and beyond the physical sphere. Beliefs and spirituality affect the life of the Anyuwaa people and their understanding of the existence of God and deities. The Anyuwaa believe in the existence of a supreme God and subordinate deities, and their lives are surrounded with superstitions.

Concept and Existence of God—Jwøk

The concept of God has a broad meaning in the Anyuwaa belief and worldview. However, the Anyuwaa people distinguish different uses of the word *jwøk* based on context and a wide-ranging worldview and concepts. As in the words of Harvey Hoekstra, the word *Jwøk* is on the lips of every Anyuwaa, and it could mean "God, the creator." A person could be a *jwøk*. An individual who was ill was said to have a *jwøk*. If one was startled, the one-word, spontaneous response was "*Jwok*."[28] This is because the word *jwøk* is used to reference different things from spirits, illness, luck, and anything stranger to the Anyuwaa is *jwøk*. Yet, the Anyuwaa know what it implies when they use *Jwøk* (*jwok* means god, spirits, and *Jwøk* represents God).

They believe in the existence of the supreme being—God. *Jwøk* has no gender. *Jwøk* is powerful (omnipotent), loving, caring and is fair in the execution of justice. *Jwøk* is limitless, lives everywhere, omnipresent as Christians would say, and remains mysterious as *Jwøk* cannot be objectified; *Jwøk* hears and sees everything, but *Jwøk* cannot be seen. Yet, rarely, *Jwøk* becomes visible through extraordinary incidents, we called miracles, because *Jwøk* is hidden behind God's own persona. When one survived a lion, a crocodile, a buffalo, etc., when a person is lost in the bush and found alive or has a near death experience, etc., the Anyuwaa

---

28. Hoekstra, *Honey, We're Going*, 113–14.

would say, "beeye Jwøk," meaning "that is God"—attributing the action to the supreme God.

As discussed above, the Anyuwaa belief attested that God ascended above the skies leaving the earth due to the increase of human disobedience and now lives transcendent in the skies. Every myth and legend places *Jwøk* above every creation. God lives in the sky, a pure sphere of God's dwelling, and earth is a human territory. This concept resembles Jesus' statement to Nicodemus when he grappled to understand earthly things and Jesus' claim that "no one has ascended into heaven except he who descended from heaven, the Son of Man" (John 3:13 ESV). I agree with Jacob K. Olupona, in order to explain this complicated worldview, that the "Africans operate with a three-dimensional perception of space: the sky, the earth (land and water), and the ancestral or spirit world, which is located under the earth."[29]

This is true for the Anyuwaa: God lives in a pure sphere and alone; however, *Jwøk* is active, though invisible, and the continuance of creation is God's presence at all moments and places, in nature and the elements. God is the "supreme spiritual power providing all things with the physical force to procreate."[30] He is only approachable when one seeks justice because only God is the right judge. The Anyuwaa believe that God intervenes in human affairs only to execute justice, and no one escapes God's absolute justice. Whenever there is a cold case, when a thief is not caught, or if one is mistreated, the Anyuwaa would say, "Jwøk nuttö, mare ongøl Jwøki," meaning "God exists and God will judge the case."

There is also the spiritual world inhabited by ancestors below the earth; only elders are close to such a sphere as they are close to the end of their life cycle in the human realm and moving toward the spiritual world of the ancestors. Also, there is the world of humans infested with misery from the gods that are lurking and dwell in the trees and lakes. For this reason, *the Anyuwaa, like other Africans, live lives in fear of spirits, always make sacrifices, and bring offerings to appease the anger of these*

---

29. Olupona, *African Sprituality*, 56.

30. Perner, *Sphere of Spirituality*, 27.

spirits. People seek protection from spirits of deities, sorcery, and the evil eye through the performance of rituals, the use of symbols, and the practice of witchcraft.

Subordinate Deities—Juu

Like Christians, the Anyuwaa traditional religious concept and worldview holds that other gods exist in this world. The Nuer, their neighboring tribe, believe in the existence of Buuk (female) and Deeng (male), the gods of rivers and of rain beside Kwoth, the supreme God of true spirit who is in the heavens. While the Nuer as a tribe *celebrate* Buuk and Deng and yet each clan might have a clan god to which they link their story, it is different with the Anyuwaa people. The Anyuwaa tribe does not have a tribal spiritual deity that the whole tribe celebrates or worships like the Nuers. No wonder Don McClure understood them as people with a "very little of any religion or religious ceremonies. . . . In fact I have never seen any of them make a prayer to their gods, although I have seen them make sacrifices."[31] This is because the people of Shulla or Shilluk, among whom Mr. McClure evangelized before moving to the Anyuwaa country, conducted communal religious ceremonies like the Nuers. The legend behind this was that when the Anyuwaa and the Shilluk separated during the Luo migration, the Shilluk retained the religious symbols and adopted their gods such as the goddess of rain, but the Anyuwaa kept the political symbols. Whatever the reason might be, the Anyuwaa as a tribe do not have a tribal god to pray nor sacrifice to.

Yet, the Anyuwaa believe in the multiplicity of subordinate gods they called *Juu*. As stated above, the Anyuwaa live in autonomous villages and each village in the Anyuwaa land has its own village god. But to Don McClure's surprise, the Anyuwaa are superstitious and make sacrifices here and there to their little village spirits (gods), as he had witnessed a typical Anyuwaa ritual performance, beliefs, and the fear associated with it as he

31. Partee, *Story of Don McClure*, 274.

described it in one of the letters, saying, "One huge old tree from which the others had started, was threatening to fall into the river, and the people were making sacrifices and placing charms to try to save it. The witch doctors had been busy with their blood and gourds. . . . They insisted that anyone who attacked a sacred tree would surely and quickly die."[32]

Every custom and everything the Anyuwaa do, is oriented around spirituality and superstition, including pregnancy, giving names to the babies, etc. It was perceived that some of these gods of other villages, such as Abulla, Dwøle¸ Odäru, Lëërö, Thattha, etc. dominate other gods and can give names beyond their territorial villages.

Regarding the names, Anyuwaa used to have three given names for the first to the third born. The first born are named Omod, Ojulu, and Obang if males, and Ariet or Amod, Ajulu, and Abang if females. Then children born after these three are given different names when the spirits give names in the form of a dream. In their custom, the Anyuwaa people used not to give names before the child was grown and parents were sure that the baby would survive. The belief surrounding delaying giving names was that gods attack younger children when they are not appeased. Therefore, Anyuwaa are not convinced to give names to a newborn until they pass certain time, and until its first birthday the baby is addressed by a nickname until is given a real name. *Juu* are dangerous during those days in Anyuwaa culture. They threaten and traumatize people as they ask for sacrifices in the form of a hen, a goat, or a cow with specific colors, and if anyone fails to fulfill such a demand, the Anyuwaa believe that the god will take a younger child in the family as a ransom. During this waiting period, a person may approach the parents stating that they had a dream from this or that village god that the name of child must be named after that god. This always comes with great prices. Parents must meet the demands of such god by giving beads or any live animal, for fear that if these requirements are not met, the gods will be angry and kill the child or deform the newborn.

32. Partee, *Story of Don McClure*, 278.

The above-mentioned gods can give names beyond their local villages. When one passes through their territories, one must follow certain rules of how to walk, point fingers, etc. and one must be careful of what they say in such territories. These gods are water or mountain deities and those dwelling in trees. They call these subordinate gods *jwøk nyodungngö*, meaning gods of extinction and God as *Jwøk Nyingøla-Buuö*, meaning Multiplicity of Life. The Anyuwaa believe that God keeps life continuous and multiplies creation and is the symbol of permanence. Therefore, in every village there is one person, recognized as the father of the land based on their lineage, who has the right to perform rituals for land, pray for safety during fishing, hunting, war and to expel bad luck in the village. They offer little rituals to allow people to fish in the lake, cross the river, etc. Also, the Anyuwaa adopted the belief of the gods of other tribes and have shrines built in their homes.

> Walking through the village, we notice that here and there are mounds of dirt with several tall sticks on the top of which are the horns of some former cow. Tied to the sticks are ears of corn. Buried beneath the mound of dirt are the fetish bones and charms and even possibly, the body of some relative who has died and is buried there. Often, as I preach in the villages, I see on either side of me these pagan shrines and known that only as Jesus comes into their hearts and transforms them will the fear and superstition that haunts our people's hearts be taken away. Often, I will ask them if the Gospel is not a good word from God (Anuaks ask a question with a particle that anticipates a positive answer) and they will answer, "It is good word." Then I ask them, "Will you not trust in Jesus, God's only son to care for you and save you." They answer that they want to, but then I point to their shrines and tell them that if they trust in Jesus, they must throw these shrines out in the field because Jesus wants them to trust in Him only. They smile and know that what Odola (that is my African name) said is true, but in their hearts, they are still afraid to do so. We can bring them just that far and then we know that we must wait for the Holy Spirit to take all fear and superstition

away and to plant within them the new life. Pray for the power of God to be released here in the heart of Africa.[33]

The fear of the village deities and their immediate vengeance toward people was a challenge for missionaries when they first came to the Anyuwaa land, and this fear has continued even today. As stated above, often new converts remain engulfed in fear thinking that the gods are lurking to take vengeance against them. *This compels us to act and demands the need for a practical discipleship model that fosters spiritual maturity for an informative faith to help respond to such beliefs*, which we will discuss more in the conclusion of this project. Now and then Anyuwaa, including Christians, have great fear of spirits, village gods, or spells of witchcraft and do their best to keep the spirits at bay or protect themselves against infestation through prayers, seeking witch doctors, etc.[34]

Witchcraft and Divination

Witchcraft is widely practiced in the Anyuwaa land and is a dominant custom exercised by witch doctors. However, there is less divination among the Anyuwaa, and Conradin Perner is right in his conclusion that "the Anyuwaa doctors do not divine, but they see a sickness by making them reflect themselves on the ground."[35] As the Anyuwaa believe in the spiritual sphere and physical territories, they also believe in the physical and spiritual nature of human beings. They believe that the spirits of *Juu* tend to invade human territory to bring diseases and cause sickness to humans' spiritual nature and that only the doctors can expel and bring healing. Therefore, the Anyuwaa witch doctors are believed to have knowledge of the human body and organs and are capable of recognizing the nature of a sickness and deciding its nature, whether it is physical or spiritual.

33. Hoekstra, *Honey, We're Going*, 64.

34. Perner, *Sphere of Spirituality*, 30.

35. Perner, *Sphere of Spirituality*, 203.

When Don William McClure, the first missionary to the Anyuwaa land, moved from Akobo at the border of Sudan to his new mission station in Pokwøw, meaning, "village of life," he saw something dramatic. On one occasion, the Reverend McClure wrote to his partners in the United States to update them about the work among the Anyuwaa people along the banks of the Opëënö in Gambella, Ethiopia. Then he mentioned in his letter an incident of an old Anyuwaa woman coming to Christ as people made public professions of faith during a public service and said,

> An old, old woman (possibly fifty-five years old) also shaking with fright asked to speak. She had in her hand an old gourd that rattled as she shook it, and she held it up, saying, "This has been my Jwøk, and sometimes it has been my Anaka [Satan]. If I wanted something, it was my god, but if I wanted to curse someone, it was my devil. I wanted now to give it up and worship only Jesus." Again, we sang and prayed, but this time with even more enthusiasm.[36]

What the woman has said is the basic understanding of witchcraft and witch doctors in the Anyuwaa culture. Like other Africans, the Anyuwaa believe in the power of witch doctors. One person is believed to have the power to cast both evil spells and curative spells. They function as agents of good, giving hope, and restoring health and fortunes, but on the other hand, play the devils, *anägö* in Dha-Anyuwaa, meaning "the one that kills." The person, such as the woman in Mr. McClure's story, can multitask based on circumstances, personal needs, and concerns. Yet, one thing must be clear for our outside readers. A witch doctor can cast evil spells, cure, or heal sickness and expel curses but cannot curse someone.

Curse, *aciëni* in Dha-Anyuwaa, is an evil spell cast on someone but only takes effect upon the speller's death. A curse does not involve sorcery, but plain words spoken to the higher God, the absolute judge. And the same is said of blessings or last will, *gwiëth*. At midnight, early in the morning, or when alone on a road, an elderly Anyuwaa speaks pure words presenting the case

36. Partee, *Story of Don McClure*, 287.

to God. In the case of mistreatment, they would ask God to judge and bring misery on the person they are cursing, if the case is approved on their side. Or ask for blessing on someone or their children, that God bestow on them a certain kind of blessing when they pass on. This practice involves a lifetime repetition of the same case over and over believing that the mount of words piled up is unambiguous evidence of the truth of the case presented. Yet there are also blessings that can be conferred during the lifetime of the conferrer and take effects on the individual wished for, and rarely, the same can be said of a curse.

In their exercise of investigation, most often the witch doctors use leatherstrips, "wac thöör" in Dha-Anyuwaa.

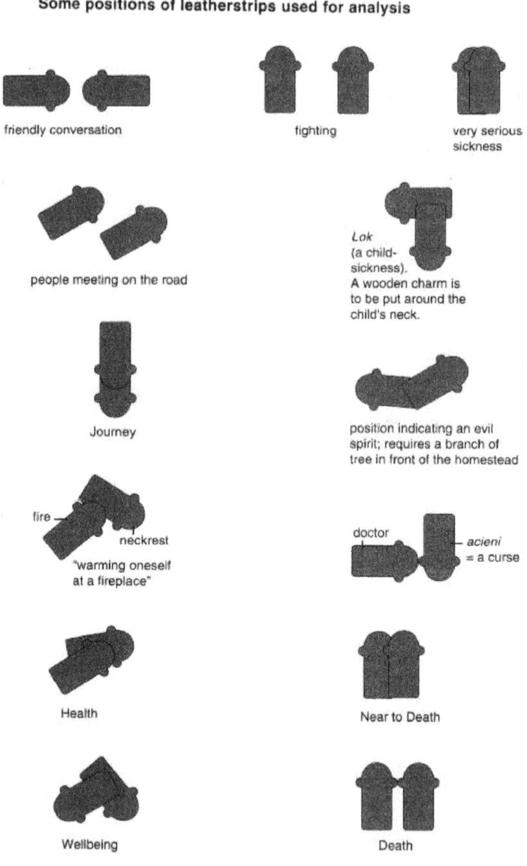

Witch doctors analyze the positions of the leatherstrips in order to pinpoint where the problem lies.

Then the witch doctors interpret the position of the leatherstrips to discover the cause of the sickness, misfortune, or infertility before they recommend the possible means to cure or expel it.

In this regard, people seek the service of witch doctors to read their fortune, to cut the tie of a curse or bewitchment when they think that they might have been cursed by an elder whom they might have mistreated when that elder was still alive. Or perhaps an enemy might have cast an evil spell on them. The same witch doctor can cast a spell on someone, bringing misfortune to that person when approached by someone who wishes their enemies bewitched.

Therefore, witch doctors practice sorcery to bewitch someone when they act on their evil side but also have the power to cure sickness, expel spirits, and countrast curses that have infected an individual's spiritual state. After their determination, they might prescribe roots, leaves, or charms for healing if the sickness is merely physical but might demand blood sacrifice of an animal or a hen to cure or repel a curse in the case of spiritual sickness. They also use a practice called *kwath* meaning "fanning away" by applying certain tree leaves and fire smoke to drive out spirits from the body and spiritual state of a person. They believe that early evenings are the perfect time for fanning away spirits, and as the darkness looms, the spirit, or *jwiëy*, can vanish unseen into the dark when exiting the body. As Conradin Perner stated, the Anyuwaa witch doctors are believed to have "inherited or acquired both knowledge of the human body and a magical power to cure diseases and who has entered into contact with spiritual matters; though the doctor cannot dominate these spiritual matters, he does not need to fear them and therefore can find the evil in a body or mind and expel it by different means."[37]

37. Perner, *Sphere of Spirituality*, 202.

Divination: Anyuak doctors trying to find the cause of a disease.

However, a renowned witch doctor named Oman, who had given up his witchcraft for Christ, once exposed the secret of sorcery, and disputed the claim of its effectiveness and clarity. He held that even if there might be truth in their practice, witch doctors cheat and mislead people all the time, and the simple words spoken by the witch doctors during their sorcery are no more powerful and effective than the words said by an average person toward the spiritual sphere or spiritual world of deities.

Prayers and Healing

Prayer and healing play a vital role in the Anyuwaa cultural practice. For the Anyuwaa people, healing is restoring the right of health and well-being perverted by sickness, infertility, and misfortune, and healing is accomplished primarily through words of prayer. The Anyuwaa word for "prayer" is *lam*, a word and concept that already existed in their language and was extended to also mean "prayer" in Christian context. The Anyuwaa people believe in spoken words and *lam* means speaking plain words commanding the spirits to leave the body. When an Anyuwaa runs out of options, including seeking insights and healing from witch doctors, they turn to their words. They believe that words have the power to repel curses, to pronounce blessings, and to heal sickness.

The Anyuwaa people perceive those spirits invading human territory and affecting people both as individuals and at the corporate level. In case of corporate incidents, the father of the land prays for the well-being of the village, the safety of hunters, fishermen, and the fortune of youth. For the Anyuwaa on the Opëënö River, the father of the land collects water from the center of the river and keeps the water in a special gourd. They would take a fresh leaf of a certain tree, and, early in the morning, they would dip the leaf in the water, tap on the wound while asking for cure and healing. This is always done when someone is hurt during hunting, war, or fishing. Then the father of the land would say, "ni näk ngøøpi ngøøp kwara døøc, bäng gïn tägï dëëri" (if this land is of my ancestors, nothing will happen to you)—affirming that the person will not die but be healed from the injuries.

Another practice for healing is spitting. Spitting a light saliva on a wound is believed to have power to heal, as in the story of the blind man in John 9. Spitting is also used as a form of warm welcome and a blessing conferred by an elder relative. When a young person comes back from a trip or to visit a relative, an elder spits on the head of the young person as their best way to welcome them and wish them an enjoyable time.

When there is epidemic in the area, villages in the same territory conduct a ceremony called *Pöö*, a corporate chasing of spirits from one village to another with burning torches and the repeating of words denouncing the invasion, saying *cii mari ëë, cii mari ëë*, literally, "go with what is yours," asking the spirit to leave the village, taking the sickness with it. They would go throughout every corner of the village with burning torches, while beating objects and making noise to exorcise the spirits lurking and supposedly hanging in the closets of huts of the village. Lastly, they would throw those objects into the river, and as they floated away with the stream, it was viewed as a sign of the departure of the bad spirits. This no less than the sacrifice of Jesus and the ministry of the apostles driving out demons by the name of Jesus, where human beings are healed from curses and freed from demonic spirits (Matt 26:27–28; Luke 11:14–26; Acts 19).

Lastly, the Anyuwaa believe in an individual prayer. Though informal, compared to other types of prayer, individual Anyuwaa ask God the right to own something. When hunting or fishing, they ask God that it is their legitimate right to catch a fish or kill an animal to survive. They ask for protection, good health, and luck because only God can supply such things, and it is the right thing for God to provide for them.

Concept of Death and the Afterlife

The Anyuwaa believe in existence after this current life and in two types of death: natural or human made, the latter involving a curse or bewitchment by a witch or an evil eye. Whether an individual died by a gunshot, being hit by a spear, an animal attack, in an accident, or because of a persistent illness, the Anyuwaa always find a way to understand the death by consulting a witch doctor to determine the cause of death. The Anyuwaa of the Opëënö River used a unique practice to determine whether someone died a natural death or because of human involvement. They opened the grave during the same season as when the individual had died. For example, if a person died in a summer of this year, they opened the grave in the summer of the third year. If the body was not found in the grave—maybe it had decayed—such person was believed to have died a natural death and been taken to God's realm. However, if the body did not decompose, they would say the cause was not natural, and then the family would seek the insight of a witch doctor to investigate the cause. They would not attack a person who was suggested by the witch doctor, but an elder relative would take the matter and present the case to God, asking God to intervene and judge the case.

However, whatever type of death a person died, the general belief is that soul never dies and when a person dies, he or she transitions and dwells in the ancestral world, passing from the human realm to the spiritual world. This means that death activates a person's spiritual nature and "the passage enhances the spiritual powers so that one could now operate in the human environment and especially in the human family as a guardian, protective spirit/power/influence."[38] Those who left the physical world are now living as spirits but live among the people. They demand respect and the performance of certain rituals. When they appear in dreams, they ask for offerings in the form of a fermented drink called *ogweea*, which is to be poured on their grave. *Ogweea* is a special drink offering, given to strengthen the relationship between the departed soul and those still in the human world. The Anyuwaa Bible translators were accurate in using Paul's statement to the Philippians, when he said he would greatly rejoice with them if he were being poured like a drink offering to enhance their faith (Phil 2:17).

The other concept of the continuation of the soul is the incarnation or transformation. The Anyuwaa believe in the continuation of life through reincarnation of the soul to certain animals associated with the person's soul. Based on family background, a person's soul can turn into a lion, a snake, a lizard, etc. Lastly, life continues by being born again to a family member. A person dies, their body may decay but the soul is recreated or regenerated and sent back to this world in the body of a different person, born as a child of a close family member. If the newborn resembles an old relative, the Anyuwaa believe that such a person has returned.

Likewise, the immortality of soul is also symbolized by placing a fresh *gëëwö* branch at the edge of a grave at burial because *gëëwö* takes root and grows easily when placed in the ground. In general, the Anyuwaa concept of the immortality of the soul reflects on the truth of the Bible that death is a sleep and a means of transition to the realm of God (Dan 12:2; Matt 9:24; 1 Thess 4:13–18).

---

38. Olupona, *African Spirituality*, 54.

Missionaries in the Anuak Country

As mentioned above in the introduction of the book, the word of God and the light of hope came to the Anyuwaa country through a Pennsylvania native by the name of Don William McClure of Blairsville, Pennsylvania. Don and Lyda McClure came to the Anyuwaa people from the Akobo of Sudan. They worked among the Anyuwaa and expanded their territory to the east of the Opëënö River of Gambella, Ethiopia, between 1938 and 1950.[39] Don and Lyda had evangelized the Shilluk people in the west and heard about the Anyuwaa at the border. As stated above, this was the period of high tensions between the Anyuwaa with the Ethiopian government and the Anyuwaa in Akobo with the Sudan government. Don McClure's first task was to "explore the territory along the upper reaches of the Sobat, Baro [Opëënö], Pibor, and Akobo Rivers to learn more about the Anuaks and to choose a location from which he would best minister to them."[40]

In the years that followed, the McClures would start their mission at Akobo, build huts for themselves and start gospel work. They found the Anyuwaa "to be wonderfully friendly and likable."[41] Mr. McClure's plan was to evangelize and bring the Anyuwaa people to Christ in fifteen years. To implement his proposal, Don McClure was to energize his fellow Americans to support his work and respond to his invitation so that missionaries with different areas of expertise could come collaborate with him in Africa. Mr. McClure wanted "to concentrate a large staff of fifteen missionary units in three different areas of Anuak territory [and] in each there would be five missionaries with a combined expertise in evangelism, medicine, agriculture, and education. They would work on preaching and Bible translation, public health, food production, literacy training, building, and economic development."[42] His vision for the Anyuwaa church was

---

39. Partee, *Story of Don McClure*, 141.

40. Partee, *Story of Don McClure*, 142.

41. Partee, *Story of Don McClure*, 146.

42. Partee, *Story of Don McClure*, 151–52.

to establish a complete independent church that is self-sustaining (economically); self-propagating (in mission and discipleship); and self-governing (in leadership).[43]

Don McClure was successful in large part. His mission frontier extended to Pokwøw and Gilø in Gambella, Ethiopia, besides the Akobo station in Sudan. Missionaries with different skills and talents joined Don and Lyda McClure. Among those were Niles and Ann Reimer, who remained great friends of the Anyuwaa even after the missionaries were expelled from both Ethiopia and Sudan. The first schools and clinics in Gambella were opened by the Presbyterian missionaries. Harvey Hoekstra, with a group of young Anyuwaa learners, managed to translate the New Testament into the Anyuwaa language, and the first prints of the Bible came on the same day, January 10, 1962, as the MAF (Mission Aviation Fellowship) airplane that came to pick them out of Akobo when they were expelled.

> The pilot handed me a small package. He said, "You'll probably want to open this before you leave." When I opened that package, inside it [was] the first five printed, beautifully bound copies of the Anuak New Testament. We handed them out to the Anuaks who were there and could read. We will never forget the words of one of the men as he said, "Our hearts (livers) are heavy as you go away, but you are leaving behind God's best gift. You have given us His word in our language."[44]

Harvey left the Bible as a gift for the Anyuwaa people, and it was indeed a priceless gift. The Anyuwaa continued using Harvey's translation until June of year 2010 when the whole Bible was translated into the Anyuwaa language.

43. Partee, *Story of Don McClure*, 152.
44. Hoekstra, *Honey, We're Going*, 189.

Mission Opportunities and Setbacks

The Anyuwaa frontier was untapped territory presenting an opportunity for evangelism and education during the 19th and early 18th centuries. Though there were ethnologists and anthropologists who had trodden this unknown region in the prior years for research purposes, neither the Sudan nor the Ethiopian governments had offered education nor evangelized the Anyuwaa people. According to Carl Templin (Keerø), Don McClure had one of his first encounters with the Anyuwaa people through the students from Akobo who were attending school in Doleib Hill Mission School among the Shulla or Shilluk.[45] Don McClure noticed a few students at the school who were speaking a slightly different dialect than the Shilluk's language. As mentioned above, the Anyuwaa and Shilluk, or Coole (PL) in Dha-Anyuwaa, are close relatives tracing their ancestral father to one person—Chwezi or Cwääy. However, they had separated and lived apart during the great migration.[46]

When Reverend Don McClure learned about this ethnic group living eastward of his mission territory, he was interested in evangelizing the Anyuwaa people. However, Don McClure had to present his new project to the Presbyterian General Assembly for approval and to gain support for a new mission project. Sadly, the General Assembly refused to fund this new project. In his persistence, Reverend McClure asked the General Assembly for permission to raise money for this mission project. After such permission and with his gift of speech, Don McClure managed to win the hearts of Americans to support his work. Monetary support for all missionaries to the Anyuwaa land came from the funds and generosity collected through his speeches. The leaders of the church disapproved Reverend McClure's request on the suspicion of money embezzlement from the general fund, but the fact was that the leaders were jealous of Don McClure's success in his mission work in Africa. Therefore, the Anyuwaa project was a special project funded specifically by the money raised from local

45. Carl Templin, interview by author, Nov 23, 2011.

46. Shillington, *History of Africa,* 118–19.

churches and businesspersons, not from the Presbyterian Mission Fund. "Without Odaan [the Anyuwaa name for Don] you wouldn't be a pastor today," said Carl Templin.[47]

The Reverend Carl Templin is right. Many of us in the ministry today have profound respect for our missionaries who gave up their American life and chose to dwell among the Anyuwaa people, an area without any infrastructure at the time. The Anyuwaa land was an open field for mission and the opportunity to introduce a new God and new way of worship was highly needed. The story of Odhieng Omod, the father of the Reverend John Odhieng, reflects such longing for God among the Anyuwaa people. In his story, Odhieng was asking his friends whether it was possible to know God. His villagers told him not to attempt to know God, because people who try to know God tend to go crazy. As said above, the Anyuwaa put God above the skies in God's own pure sphere. They have village gods whom they can learn to appease through a variety of activities and rituals, as mentioned previously. It was easier to do so than to seek to know God. The Anyuwaa think in attempting to know or deeply think about knowing God, a person experiences psychosis and hallucinations, losing contact with the real world.

Luckily, Odhieng had heard about certain people in Pokwøw (that was the second mission station besides Akobo) who knew God and could teach people to attain knowledge about God. He decided to pursue his dream and travel hundreds of miles to Pokwøw, in the Gambella, Ethiopia, area from the Pochalla area in Sudan. Odhieng came to Pokwøw at the time the missionaries were constructing the clinic, the church building, and missionary homes and Don McClure had required the workers to go to worship in the morning before they resumed work. Among the hired Anyuwaa was the recent arrival, Odhieng Omod.

> Odhieng said the first time he heard about God in the morning sermon he came to know God and within a week he joined the literacy group with the primer prepared by Harvey Hoekstra, and he managed to read the primer easily. He went back to Sudan and in 1965 when we went

47. Carl Templin, interview by author, Nov 23, 2011.

> back to Pinyudo mission station [the third mission station], we found Odhieng. He had moved his family to Pinyudo due to the civil war in Sudan. While he remained as a successful farmer, he was an amazing layperson serving the church and later moved back to Sudan.[48]

There is also the story of the Reverenced Akway Ochudho, a fine man who became the first evangelist, then pastor among the entire Anyuwaa tribe. As Harvey Hoekstra stated, he met a young Anyuwaa when he returned to Pokwøw as Reverend Don McClure took his long furlough to the United States. Harvey Hoekstra came to Gambella early on to start the mission station after Don McClure secured the permission to evangelize the Anyuwaa. During one of those trips from Akobo to Gambella, Mr. Hoekstra had given a small book to a young Norwegian who at the time was serving with the Bank of Ethiopia, and with him was an Anyuwaa servant. At his return, he found this young man reading a mimeographed copy of the First Epistle of John at the mission station. "He looked up and said, 'You don't remember me. But I remember you. When you were in Gambella several years ago with another man you called Bomb, you ate supper at the home of the man I was working for. . . . Before you left, you gave a little book to this man. With that book, he taught me to read. When Odan came here, I learned more about Jesus and was baptized.'"[49] The Anyuwaa land and their hearts were ripe and ready to be harvested for the Lord's kingdom.

Being a hidden region more isolated than the rest of the world, the Anyuwaa land presented a wonderful opportunity for evangelism. But it was also susceptible to the influence of Islam. In fact, the contribution of hundreds of pounds by Aga Khan of India to Islamize the Anyuwaa through Sudan provided the impetus for Emperor Haile Selassie of Ethiopia to give Don McClure permission to bring Christianity to the Anyuwaa people.[50]

48. Carl Templin, interview by author, Nov 23, 2011.

49. Carl Templin, interview by author, Nov 23, 2011. See also Hoekstra, *Honey, We're Going*, 139.

50. Partee, *Story of Don McClure*, 243.

And Don McClure was successful using education and healthcare opportunities to draw Anyuwaa to God.

However, in the Anyuwaa country in the 1900s, setbacks were inevitable. The Anyuwaa church did not expand to villages, and one could say that Christianity remained in the mission stations. There are four reasons that hindered the success of the Anyuwaa missions: First were the regional government bureaucratic routines that had delayed the opening of the first mission station among the Anyuwaa in Gambella. Missionary personnel had to travel back and forth from Akobo to Gambella, and the government officials were hard to convince and accepted the letter from their senior bosses in Addis Ababa.[51] Also, the expulsion of the missionaries from both Sudan and Ethiopia has contributed to this challenge.

Second was that the use of the Amharic alphabet instead of the Latin letters was a great challenge both for the trainers and learners. In Akobo, the missionaries had already introduced the Latin alphabet, and young Anyuwaa learned to read using Latin letters. At that time, the Bible translation was underway by Harvey Hoekstra and a small group of Anyuwaa students, and the primers to teach reading skills were prepared. However, the government of Ethiopia disapproved the use of Latin letters to help educate the Anyuwaa of Ethiopia at Pokwøw mission station. Therefore, due to the Ethiopian government's refusal to permit the use of Latin alphabetical letters, Dr. James Keefer (Oman Cham, his Anyuwaa name) and Omod Okoony tried to transliterate the premiers previously written using Latin letters to the Amharic letters—*fidel.* The teachers from Sudan had to learn a new language, Amharic, to teach language primers to develop reading skills.

In this regard, it was a slow process to train evangelists, and Carl Templin remembers Daniel Gora from Sudan, a great hunter who had only a couple of years of education. He served as an evangelist in Gilo mission station church and had only two sermons throughout the year: the story of creation and John 3:16.[52] Such was the impact caused by the government into the illiteracy of

---

51. Hoekstra, *Honey, We're Going,* 139–40.

52. Carl Templin, interview by author, Nov 23, 2011.

the Anyuwaa people. Until today, discipleship murkiness in the Anyuwaa church can be linked to lack of faith formation materials and how it was started. On the other hand, history remains true, and we are all in debt to the remarkable contribution of the young Anyuwaa educators from Akobo Sudan to the evangelism and literacy of the Anyuwaa of Ethiopia.

Third was the response of the missionaries to address cultural practices and traditional norms of their converts. It was what the great author of Nigeria Chinua Achebe reflected on in his book *Things Fall Apart*,[53] indicating missionaries' failure to recognize common human qualities of the natives they were evangelizing. Things fell apart due to the missionaries' negative view of the Anyuwaa natives, referring to them as "a person with small mind like a child."[54] Rigidity and barring polygamists from baptism or urging them to divorce one of their wives can also be mentioned as part of the hesitancy of the Anyuwaa to accept Christianity.[55] New converts are also forbidden to drink locally fermented alcohol, and if one was found drinking, it was said that the missionaries would dispose the drink as a punishment. Since the Anyuwaa share such local provisions, people would be offended by such acts. Also, missionaries seemed to fail to embed the Anyuwaa worldview, beliefs, and positive cultural practices into gospel preaching. In response, the natives considered this religion as trespasser.

Fourth was unmet needs and the power of the culture over the converts and evangelists. At first, the evangelists had had trainings with fully funded accommodations. Yet, as the mission funds dwindled, so did funding for meals at the school. To resolve the issue, the missionaries suggested a Theological Education by Extension (TEE), where evangelists completed more study on their own and came back only for group study during certain times of the year. However, the evangelists resisted such an education system, wanting a more formal and regular theological system for better understanding. In disappointment, enough evangelists abandoned

53. Achebe, *Things Fall Apart*, 209.
54. McClure, *Red-Headed*, 96.
55. Hoekstra, *Honey, We're Going*, 177.

their commitment and went back to their own villages. Once the evangelists found themselves surrounded by their traditional practices, many of them returned to these practices. As a result, many of them became polygamists and ashamed of preaching about a god who does not accept polygamists, divorcees, and those who consume locally fermented alcohols.

Therefore, the spread of Christianity became limited to the mission stations and some pockets of villages here and there in Opëënö and Gilo with only a few worshipers. Anyuwaa traditions and cultural practices seemed to have mounted pressure on the small number of believers of the time. People were afraid of the witch doctors, village gods, and curses of the elders; traditional dances and stick fights were widely practiced.[56] Also, chiefs often charged youths of their own villages with responsibilities. And when you are a Christian convert and told to avoid such activities or move away from the village to the mission stations, the chief punishes your father and requires a goat, a lamb, or a bull to compensate for your absence. So, pressured by such responses, Christians go back to their villages to resume village duty in order to restore honor and respect of their families.

Those who sought medical services would accept Jesus Christ, but only for the time when they were around missionaries at the mission stations. They would abandon their faith when they got back to their respective villages. Christianity and the gospel messages were ignored, and gospel proclamation could not stand in the face of the Anyuwaa tradition and worldviews. Throughout this period, Christianity became something to be ashamed of and was left only for the neglected and the laziest people in the society until at the turn of the decade and the regime change in Ethiopia in 1991.

> These were old days, Owar, and what I see now among
> your people, yes it was a slow process but, in some ways,
> the Dergue regime [Ethiopian communist regime] made
> us leave and that the Anuak would assume the leadership

---

56. Hoekstra, *Honey, We're Going*, 137.

by themselves. That was the purpose of the Anyuwaa church to have the church that is self-governing[57]

The Reverend Carl Templin's message confirms the fulfillment of the Reverend Don McClure's prophetic vision for the Anyuwaa church. Therefore, it remains for the Anyuwaa church to carry the torch from our great missionaries, *yet with the transformative and restorative message to help our members understand God and the purpose of sending Jesus for our salvation. It is possible to know God and if we are crazy, then we are crazy because he has revealed himself to us.* Knowing God matters. It is the purpose of the discipleship process. It helps us teach the doctrine of God, emboldened like Peter, who answered who Jesus is. Such knowledge drives out fear of the local gods, weakens the power of the witch doctors and the desire to seek their services. Knowing God and how Jesus' death on the cross affects our salvation and how this relates to the work of the Holy Spirit through us, the function of the church in the world, and our destiny in Christ's return is explained through the discipleship process.

Now, as members of the Anyuwaa society, we can strive to embed our worldview and contextualize our belief stories to create a working discipleship model that can foster spiritual maturity in our churches. As Anthony J. Gittins said, "If we forget our stories, we will forget who we are; and without a strong identity we will be unable to function as the people of God."[58]

57. Carl Templin, interview by author, Nov 23, 2011.

58. Gittins, *Reading the Clouds*, xv.

CHAPTER 4

Insights for Effective Approaches to Fostering Discipleship

> Nothing is gained either by failing to recognize signs of common grace in culture or by reading the gospel into cultural texts where it is not present. Only when we truly understand what is happening around us can we engage our world intelligently and effectively (and evangelistically).[1]

THIS WELL-ARTICULATED STATEMENT AFFIRMS the importance of deploying a methodology that pursues understanding of worldview, contextual elements, tradition, and as a result may reward us with the finest resources that will give us deliverable practice. In this regard, when we finally come to our understanding of our context, we begin to discern what is unfolding around us, which helps us engage positively, determined to bring change into our practices and aligned approaches. Likewise, this study methodology has assumed to investigate the overall aspects of the challenges of discipleship, church practices, culture, and the Anyuwaa tradition. It is our hope that this project enlightens our

---

1. Vanhoozer, *Everyday Theology*, 55.

understanding of the impact of the culture, tradition, and the impending challenges in our churches.

Therefore, producing an equitable questionnaire has helped capture the scope of the project aim. The interviews and group discussion have proved the importance of this project and are regarded as enlightening. Despite denominational perspectives, all the participants agreed and recognized the lack of discipleship and imbalance in church growth. Across the conversations, three things kept emerging from the discussion: lack of biblical or faith-based teachings, limited biblical knowledge, and scarcity of discipleship resources written in the Anyuwaa language. Other issues, such as absence of coordinated effort between churches and lack of denominational bylaws, are contributing factors to the existing inadequate discipleship approach in the Anyuwaa church.

Moreover, despite the strong worship commitment in all the churches and slight witness in faith growth, and the unity between individual church members, this project study has discovered the impact of the Anyuwaa culture, tradition, witchcraft, and sorcery as the dominant constraints in the lives of the members of the Anyuwaa church. And seamlessly, many agreed that the cause can be traced to a lack of discipleship teachings and faith formation practices. Many denominations do not have a formal catechism process, nor structured discipleship and faith formation programs.

Much can also be said of the lack of written resources in the language. The issue of language was one of the setbacks for mission and discipleship in the Anyuwaa church, mentioned elsewhere in this book. The Latin alphabet, which previously was prohibited by the emperor to train the Anyuwaa and translate the Bible into their language, was reintroduced in the schools in 1994 after the change of the Dergue regime in Ethiopia. Consequently, the whole Bible was not translated into Dha-Anyuwaa and made available to the people until June 2010. Thus, for the past forty-eight years, since January 1962, the Anyuwaa church was using only the New Testament Bible, which was translated using the Amharic alphabet.[2] They have been using this Bible translation as a sole resource for

2. Hoekstra, *Honey, We're Going*, 189.

teachings in the church. Only a few educated church leaders may use either Amharic or English Bibles for references. The rural Anyuwaa church depends on the Anyuwaa New Testament Bible only. However, with the regime change and the reintroduction of the Latin letters, the Anyuwaa were now required to learn a new language and the whole Bible was then translated using Latin letters.

In this transition, problems were inevitable. In the proceeding years, after the introduction of the use of the Latin alphabet, a literacy program was initiated, but did not achieve much in way of transforming the literacy skills of the people. Except for school textbooks, there have not been any spiritual materials produced or translated to Anyuwaa to help with teaching. Churches are still using the plain Holy Bible (meaning the regular Bible without study notes or commentary to guide) and/or maybe some, if any, old primers prepared by missionaries more than fifty years ago. As one of the pastors said, "Using a plain Holy Bible may help or it may be important, but without biblical education, this Bible becomes a chemistry, a physics, a geography and can turn into something else."[3] *He is right. Biblical literatures need a hermeneutical interpretation of literary texts to better understand historical contexts as well as theological implications.* Likewise, the absence of coordination and partnership between churches has hastened the impact of the discipleship crisis among the churches in Gambella.

Thus, in addition to the preceding summary, let us narrow the results to the specific questions and briefly present the main findings and encourage the reader to consider reviewing the verbatim from focus group discussion and question reflections in Appendix II.

Church Migration and Dropout

When it comes to the question and the reason for members switching churches or giving up faith, both the study group and the interviewees agreed on the existence of the problem. They also

3. Omo Okwori Ochudho, interview by author, Jun 10, 2021.

linked the problem to lack of understanding of faith and biblical truth regarding our redemption through Christ Jesus. While they acknowledged mass conversion and rapid church growth, there is mass dropout or an experience that members randomly migrate from church to another. Sadly, individual members go from one church to another without proper or formal transfer. And such individuals are accepted into membership without providing a letter of release or clearance from the church or denomination of which they were once a member. Then these people assume ecclesiastical responsibility in their new church and would do the same when they move on to a different denomination. Contrarily, the receiving church does not have any mechanism to evaluate the person's faith and commitment to Jesus Christ.

Pastors agreed that this flow of members has created a big problem in the church of the Anyuwaa. The movement is highly occurring in the towns and cities, mostly in the churches in the city of Gambella. Even if the reason cannot be tied to one issue, illiteracy, lack of biblical teaching, and absence of such knowledge are prime reasons in this crisis. The majority of believers cannot read the Bible—mostly the older generation and rural inhabitants. People leave because they do not understand what they are believing or their denomination's theology and doctrine. Many think that all the Anyuwaa churches are the same because they do not see any liturgical differences or any form of alterations from another. Yet, churches and denominations do not cooperate. And regrettably, there is a membership race. Churches want to have more members. In the murkiness of such practice, some evangelists stalk active members of other churches to lure them to their own churches. Therefore, evangelists and prophets use the disunity between churches and move between denominations, and in their departure, they take their followers with them.

When it comes to the Anyuwaa church in the Diaspora, unlike Gambella, in the Americas, members leave because of conflicts. As a result, people cease attending their fellowship services conducted in Dha-Anyuwaa to attend services in English even if most of them have limited knowledge of English language. And as it is said above, people lack understanding of the biblical truth. While there is a lack of full-time pastors that can take the teaching job seriously, everyone agrees that to tackle this problem that has been unsolved for many years in the Anyuwaa church, there must be an organized teaching that is aimed at faith growth and spiritual formation to build a stable commitment for actions in Christian life in the church.

Witch Doctors, Sorcery, and Bewitchment

It was my sincere intention to pose this question in the questionnaire to investigate the fact about my concerns over witch doctors and their influence on the members of the Anyuwaa church. This is because a question kept lingering in my mind, not over the existence of witch doctors in the Anyuwaa society, but whether Christians should seek their services. On one of the evenings in 1998, while I was leaving a choir practice, I was accompanied by a young woman. While we were walking, we kept conversing and touched on fear. Suddenly, she said in Dha-Anyuwaa, "Cer Jwøk manya køny, këël ajwøøa dhaanhnhø cøøa baange," which literally means, "God's hand needs to be assisted, you can even go to a witch doctor to assist in safeguarding a person." I did not take her seriously and did not pay attention to her statement, partially because I thought she was teasing. Yet, as I looked back, her voice kept bringing questions when rumors kept emerging in the last few years about witch doctors and experiences among the members of Anyuwaa church both in Gambella and in the Americas.

It is a heart-wrenching shock to hear that in the twenty-first century and in an era when the church has been established for over seventy years in the Anyuwaa land, some Christians would still seek the service of witch doctors, afraid of being bewitched, or attempt to approach a witch doctor to cast misfortune on their enemies. There is no better way to describe this than how one of the pastors puts it, that "people are living double minded. They are in faith but still believe and follow things of the tradition.

When they seek help, they follow the advice of others and then they seek the counsel of witch doctors."[4]

While no one has firsthand witness, all the participants in the group discussion as well as the interviewees concur that they had heard the rumors of members going to witch doctors when they face hardships, either financial or when a sickness persisted. Mostly women. A woman would seek the advice of witch doctors when their child has illness that persisted. Many think that such illness is an "Anyuwaa thing," meaning it cannot be cured medically but only by any traditional means, and that includes finding herbs and going to a witch doctor. In this case, mothers are advised to seek the service of witch doctors. The study found that many diasporas are encouraged to travel to Gambella when they have a mental health crisis or ask a relative to consult a witch doctor on their behalf. Apparently, such things are secret and cannot be shared, let alone to a pastor, but cannot be buried from being heard.

Likewise, many church members believe that an individual can cast evil spells on them. As such, some of the results are seen displayed in the church. As a customary practice, Anyuwaa people used to fear witch doctors. And these days, those who claim themselves as prophets have taken the space of witch doctors in the churches and members fear, revere them, and people lived their lives filled with fear. Therefore, prophets played their messages in those vulnerable hearts where many people submitted to their demands. Sadly, they demand money for their services, yet it is hard to convince members to stop following these prophets.

Village Gods, Tradition, and Superstitions

Without hesitation, members of the study group and interviewees responded to the question regarding fear and practice of village gods. They strongly agreed that such beliefs are diminishing in the community as well in the church. And that includes the practice

4. Ojulu Omod, interview by author, Jun 10, 2021.

of the foreign gods the Anyuwaa adopted in the past from their neighboring tribes of Nuer, Manjang, and Murle tribes.

However, the members of the study group concur in one accord on the existence of fear, superstition, and the practice of traditional rituals that are still lingering in the community, and in many incidents Christian believers are trapped in such practices. Church members are involved in *bak*, a custom/tradition by which a deceased is exchanged by an animal and is shielded with the blood of the animal. *Bak* is a shedding of the blood of an animal in the place of a deceased human being to purify them as they depart human territory. As part of this burial ritual, the blood of the animal is mixed with part of the dirt that was removed when digging the grave. This mixture serves to seal the grave after the body has been laid to rest and the grave filled in. This is considered to be an honored burial. They follow this custom even if the deceased is a believing person, or believers themselves do this to honor their family members or relatives.

Secondly, many young, pregnant women are believed to be following the custom called *okïrï*. It is a ritual performed to appease or calm the gods or spirits in order to not cause harm to an individual or unborn babies. In this case, the parents of a young girl ask the husband or his parents to provide them with a goat or sheep and beads. The animal will be slaughtered, and its blood sprinkled on the young girl and/or its small intestine tied to the waist of the girl. This ritual is also applied to girls who are experiencing infertility. The father asks that the ancestors intervene in such a crisis. He would say a few words in affirmation that the girl is indeed from his blood and from the family line. Therefore, any spirit of infertility or anything that causes childlessness must not have power over the girl.

Likewise, the study shows that many children are seen wearing beads as bracelets, in the Anyuwaa churches in Gambella. While most bracelets are worn simply for personal beauty, countless of "those beads are associated with superstitions of old way of life and demands of village gods. They encourage people to supply such things because they believe that the village god would attack and cause sickness to the child."[5]

Thirdly, the study found that mostly young men are turning to *kunjuure* (PL). *Kunjuur* (SG) is some sort of stems of plants that people wear and believe to have power to protect an individual from harm. Either they harvest or buy such stems and wear them during tribal conflicts in the belief that they contain power that can expel harm, bad luck, and/or that they exude fortune.

This is puzzling. We are not certain whether the Anyuwaa church members understand the meaning of blood. Or the village shrine's physical existence is destroyed, yet superstitions and fear toward the gods still live on in the Anyuwaa hearts. Complicitly, with all these indications, we can conclude that "there are people who still believe in such things of tradition, and we can also add into suspicion that people are still believing in the village gods as well."[6]

Polygamy among Devout Christians

Polygamy has been a challenge and continues to threaten the integrity of Christianity in the Anyuwaa church. It is becoming generational. The young ones to whom the church leaders would look for leadership fall into the trap of polygamy or having mistresses. It is obvious that this crisis is not of one denomination but that all the churches in the Anyuwaa land are experiencing similar problems including the diasporas.

In this regard, the lack of discipleship resources and the absence of bylaws that help guide leaders in church ministries, have contributed to the problem. Church leaders are concerned and do not have authority to control such a trend. This is because there are individuals who are spreading false narratives about marrying multiple wives, and the church leaders are incapable of "controlling them and are marrying more than two wives."[7]

5. Darach Thatha Abwola, interview by author, Jun 10, 2021.

6. Ojulu Omod, interview by author, Jun 10, 2021.

7. Peter Agwa Ochalla, interview by author, Jun 10, 2021.

They threaten to leave the church if they are told to respect the principles of the Bible and church rules.

Faithful Christian Living

Despite all the challenges the church is facing, pastors have been seeing faithful Christian living in their respective churches. Many have seen their members demonstrating and sharing Christian love toward one another. Church members are united. They join hands to support the weak, visit the lowly, and kindly pray for one another. Most importantly, there is a great enthusiasm in participation in worship. Church members participate in all worship programs including services that are run on weekdays, Sunday services, and spiritual conferences. In addition, the Anyuwaa church has adapted to giving tithes and offerings.

Insights and Solutions

The focus group members presented constructive insights and offered suggestions about how to tackle the crisis the Anyuwaa church is facing. They witnessed their members showing more interest in worship that includes dozens of songs and dances. However, they lack attentiveness to biblical teachings. Church members have difficulty distinguishing differences between teachings and denominations. They would rather attend worship than participate in organized biblical or leadership trainings.

To bring a lasting solution, the Anyuwaa church needs to engage in biblical teaching and minimize emphasis on worship that involves singing limitless songs. Training on ecclesiastical ecumenism, organizing seminars, and encouraging pastors to train their respective members about rules and regulation are believed to bring constructive understanding in the church. It is suggested that church leaders in Gambella and the pastors in Diaspora can jointly work together to implement biblical teachings to restore the integrity of the gospel in the Anyuwaa church.

CHAPTER 5

Considerable Implications for the Church

THIS STUDY PROJECT PRESENTS considerable implications for the Anyuwaa church in general and its congregations, where an applicable discipleship approach is lacking. The following implications grew out of the overall project as the study project includes information from focus groups and interviews. A comprehensive collection of resources and extensive reading commitment from the researcher in reviewing and reading secondary resources also played a great role in defining such implications for the ministry setting of the Anyuwaa church and ministry leaders.

1. *Teach and Preach Fundamental Principles*

A major disparity that both the focus group and the interviewee have wrestled with was the absence of biblical teaching and lack of discipleship understanding in the church of the Anyuwaa. Members of the discussion group rarely indicated their participation in teachings with a discipleship focus, and they rarely conduct sessions with an emphasis on discipleship for their respective churches. This indicates that the church has a critical need for an organized and formal teaching ministry where essential tenets of our faith and biblical principles are expounded, beginning with the catechesis of new converts and spiritual formation and leadership empowerment for active members.

The Anyuwaa church must waste no time but act now, and critically think of implementing biblical teachings. The church must seriously consider ecclesiological catechesis as an important step in the aspect of faith that requires distinctive discerning action to bring changes in the church and in the life of a Christian person. Catechesis must not be taken lightly as to preparing members for membership or confirmation, but as a vital tool for the church to invest in the gospel, build trust, convert followers, and transform them into leaders who desire to do the will of their Lord (Luke 6:46). When we start catechizing, we begin to empower members and build up interest in continued learning that leads to discipleship and faith growth. Also, the church needs to apply a catechetical methodology that brings both conscious understanding and helps to enrich faith.

This is because the teaching ministry contains broader and deeper meaning and purpose. It comprises historical, Christocentric, and apocalyptic aspects. It aims to help congregations incorporate their traditions with the message of the covenant and redemptive stories that shape their lives.[1] Therefore, the church needs to aim to utilize such teaching methodology that revolves and reflects on what the congregation does in terms of relationship, practice, and narrative stories.

Teaching is an important tool to transfer literatures and faith building throughout the history of the Bible. God encouraged and demanded that the Israelites keep teaching laws and regulations and pass on such practices to succeeding generations. The rabbinic office did carry out the task of teaching the Torah and Judaism, and their scribes passed the practice through generations. Jesus did teach and preach. The apostle Paul rented a hall in Ephesus and taught practical principles of faith, where all the Jews and Greeks heard and believed the word of the Lord (Acts 19:10). And John Calvin claimed that "the church of God will never preserve itself without a

---

1. Osmer, *Teaching Ministry*, 17.

Catechism, for it is like the seed to keep the good grain from dying out, and causing it to multiply from age to age."[2]

Therefore, teaching is a vital step in the discipleship approach where the truth of the Scripture, promises of God, and purpose of the covenant are passed on to succeeding generations. This responsibility has a continual spectrum and a chronological paradigm (*biblical narratives*), as well as eschatological formation (*sanctification*). And we can all concur with Calvin, in that the most critical office in the Christian church is "that of preacher, because it shows in a unique way how God rules his church through his Word."[3]

As the study has shown, when we teach about Trinity (God the Father, the Son, and the Holy Spirit), the person of Jesus, the efficacy of the blood of Jesus Christ for our redemption, and the authority of the Bible, it will help and bring us closer to the understanding of a practical discipleship that fosters Christian maturity in the Anyuwaa church. The church must present substantial and biblical elements of our faith against witch doctors, sorcery, gods and spirits, tradition, etc. to build up formidable faith. Matters of the sanctity of marriage must be included and taught in such a curriculum, including stressing the fact that polygamy is a result of lust and self-ambition; that being single must also be respected as part of the call as many are called to marriage, and that sexual immorality outside covenantal binding, therefore, is contrary to God's redemptive purpose—it is sin. Jesus mentioned three reasons to remain single: by birth, without desire for marriage; man-made; and lastly those who choose to remain single in glorification and gratifying the will of the Lord (Matt 19:11–12; Gal 5:19–20).

The Scripture calls us to reject and flee from immorality, and the Anyuwaa culture does not condone immoral depravity. However, the Anyuwaa church is currently lacking such a position and false teachers are encouraging an irresponsible manner of Christian life (1 Cor 6:18–20). There is great lack of knowledge even about basic biblical information. Some prophets would talk about large

2. Selderhuis, *Calvin Handbook*, 206.

3. Selderhuis, *Calvin Handbook*, 330.

and minor prophets as if large prophets are greater than the minor prophets. This is because in Dha-Anyuwaa the term would refer to greater and lesser in essence, which is not the case. As a result, some prophets would then refer themselves as greater prophets and bishops, and others as minor, a claim without any background except for lack of knowledge of basic biblical principles, which can be linked to lack of teaching in the Anyuwaa church. To resolve such a deficit, the church can start with simple initiatives and build up from there: small Bible study groups, confirmation classes, seminars, spiritual conferences, and Bible schools. This will help inform and enlarge knowledge of the biblical truth and enrich the faith of the members of the church.

And truly, I conclude with Richard Robert Osmer's three basic purposes of the teaching ministry, that teaching 1) "seeks to help Christians better understand and participate in God's redemption of the world in Christ Jesus" (*initiation*); 2) "helps Christians grow in their relationship with the risen and universal Lord" (*transformation*); and 3) "orients [Christians] toward God's promised future" (*eschatological*).[4] Vital changes can occur when the church realizes the importance of such teaching. The church can adapt to a new Christian culture, can escape being bullied by traditional norms and customary practices that threaten the authenticity of the gospel, and can avoid the germ of syncretism and the whirlwind of false prophets. In so doing, the church can nurture informed disciples.

2. *Contextualization of the Gospel Message*

In a culture such as ours, one of the indispensable actions we can engage in or supply for faith formation in the discipleship approach is contextualization of ministries and church practices. In essence, contextualization is a type of theology that portrays definitive truth about God and Christianity even as viewed through thick clouds of cultural inclinations. In this regard, a practical discipleship approach aims to explore essential Christian beliefs and provides biblical foundation within the sociological and cultural

4. Osmer, *Teaching Ministry*, 16–17.

context in order to foster mature Christian life. This means that the church leaders and the Anyuwaa church in general need to read culture through the lens of the gospel and interpret the gospel within the paradigm of the culture.

Even though we are knowledgeable of our culture and able to defend the gospel's truth, the study shows that pastors tend to remain silent about this matter and leaders choose to ignore the Anyuwaa cultural rites and traditional norms lurking in the Christian church of the twenty-first century. However, as Kevin J. Vanhoozer states,

> To be a cultural agent—a person able to make his or her own mark on culture rather than simply submit to cultural programing—one needs to be culturally literate and a critical thinker. . . . Christian cultural agency = theological competence + cultural literacy + gospel performance. It is not enough simply to know doctrine; the competent disciple must also be able to read culture.[5]

In this regard, to circumvent "cultural programing," as the Anyuwaa church seems to be leaning toward, the essential step is to start interpreting the gospel utilizing contextual elements of our culture. For example, *Okïri* and *Bak* can be interpreted through the lens of the gospel as prototypes of Jesus Christ's blood. Jesus Christ is the final end of all things and the disclosure of God, the mediator, maker, and marker of the new covenant of God. He is the culmination of the law of the Jews, the wisdom of the Greeks, and the enlightening for us the gentiles, and as a result, he becomes the righteousness for all and everyone who believes (Rom 10:4). He died as a ransom by pouring out his blood on the table of God's mercy so that we are all covered and freed from fear of gods and re-silient in the face of superstitions. The cleansing power of his blood can both purify and safeguard (1 John 1:9). There is no need for *kunjuur* (Ps 23), because the blood of Christ has power to cleanse our conscience from dead works and beliefs of cultural rites and norms and deliver us to serve the living God (Heb 9:13–14 NASB).

5. Vanhoozer, *Everyday Theology*, 55.

Therefore, there is no such thing as an "Anyuwaa thing" in sickness, including mental illness, bacterial infections, and viral infections. Christ's blood is the power to heal, and his name is the mighty tower. And whatever sickness it must be can only be cured by God and through medical treatments, but not by witch doctors (John 9:2; Exod 4:11; Acts 9:11–12).

Regarding witch doctors and sorceries, the Bible has a strong message that the church must not condone such practices (Exod 22:18). As such, the Anyuwaa church needs to preach and teach strongly against this traditional custom for the sake of creating a healthy and gospel-informed Christianity in the land. However, the church can encourage renowned witch doctors who were converted to Christianity to share their testimony during spiritual conferences and seminars, people like Oman Olwødhi and Akon-taalø. Members will learn and understand that sorcerers and witches submit to the authority of God when their territory is conquered with the word of the gospel (Acts 9:13–20), as it happened in the past when Odola Wenyari, a well-known witch doctor, smashed his sorcery gourd on the ground and the people of the village "were awestruck" and believed in the power of God.[6] Could the church imply chasing away sickness and diseases as in the past in the tradition as of *Pöö*? It surely can! The church can apply the powerful name of Jesus Christ to whose power every knee shall bow (Acts 3:1–11) and apply *cii mari ëë* in the name of Jesus. In addition to their illicit activities of divination and sorcery, the Anyuwaa witch doctors in most cases prescribe herbs.[7] Therefore, to transform and bring people to a better knowledge, church leaders must educate members on the efficacy and use of prescribed medicine from healthcare workers because most pharmaceutical medicines are extracted from plants and herbs.

Other cultural practices, views, and beliefs, such as the opening of the grave to see the departure and immortality of soul, can be a glimpse of the biblical truth of the resurrection of Jesus as is affirmed by Scriptures. Also, the practice of placing a branch

---

6. Hoekstra, *Honey, We're Going*, 84–86.

7. Ojulu, "Anywaa Traditional Religion," 49.

of fresh *gëëwö* tree at the edge of the grave during burial to symbolize the immortality of soul can also be replaced by making such *gëëwö* branches into a cross shape. In doing so, we are interpreting the gospel through the paradigm of our culture. *We are sacrificing the tradition on the table of truth of the gospel and speaking the truth of life eternal through the act of the cross.* Who was *Ochudhö,* who brought kingship? Why in our tradition, must a king always be killed rather than being deposed? How could the Anyuwaa church interpret these myths and practical traditional beliefs through the lens of the gospel?

These cultural elements often reflect some divine truths as expressed in biblical explanations of the kingdom of God and Jesus. However, these truths must be interpreted through the biblical lens by applying hermeneutical analysis.

Lastly but not least, I feel sure that if the church starts substituting sermons from appeasing as stated in the context study, and blends rebuke with the gospel message, that syncretism and malign views that are threatening the authenticity of the gospel in the Anyuwaa church will begin to dwindle and a new generation of competent disciples will emerge.

3. *Cooperation and Partnership in Leadership—Discipleship*

Paul wrote to the church in Rome: "I am longing to see you so that I may impart to you some spiritual gift to strengthen you—or rather so that we may be mutually encouraged by each other's faith, both yours and mine" (Rom 1:11–12 NIV). This term of partnership has been misused and has lost its importance. When people talk about partnership, expeditiously minds rush to monetary values and material needs, which is not the case in this or any other biblical context. Rather the purpose of Paul's partnership was based on mutual understanding of authentic enrichment of soul and strengthening faith by sharing diverse spiritual gifts among one another. Partnership is the most important element in fostering faith, growth, and practical discipleship in the life of the church. It can be both individualistic and corporate. Paul partnered with the Philippians in remembrance, in holding them in his hearts, and in preaching the gospel and with Philemon in welcoming back Onesimus as a friend and a brother in Christ, and with the Ephesians in prayer (Phil 1:3–7; 4:3; Phlm 1:17; Eph 6:19). Such a faithful approach promotes practical discipleship that fosters spiritual maturity in the church of God.

This model of partnership or of any form of it is lacking in the Anyuwaa church. If pastors could have space for their discussions, conduct Bible study, pray, and partake together, their partnership would minimize the race for members and extend a perfect image of church unity. Each one could share their gifts, and as a result different insights could emerge from such discussions and be utilized in their respective churches. Besides the Anyuwaa Council of Churches, the Anyuwaa pastors in Gambella must seek a pastoral association that can provide them with a space for conversation and prayer for one another. A similar approach can be recommended for the pastors in the Diaspora. Also, as the early church, this partnership must extend beyond the Anyuwaa territory. Wherever partnership is not practiced, discipleship is lacking and results in crisis of leadership in the church of Christ. This is because discipleship is the first step to which converts and followers are transformed into potential and informed leaders for the church.

In Gambella, each denomination must strive to align its leadership system and practices with a partner for the purpose of learning and sharing traits. For example, nondenominational churches must seek a well-established, nondenominational partner and adapt to its tenets, theology, and leadership system. It can be done between the churches in Gambella or outside the region. This is because the Anyuwaa churches and its congregations are led without proper bylaws or denominational disciplinary procedures. In such practices, problems are inevitable.

For instance, as the study shows, the current leadership style seems to shelve the leadership of the pastor, permitting the Anyuwaa church elders to hijack practices and as a result weaken biblical leadership and the pastoral role. Apparently, churches are led by informal and institutionally unauthorized statements and quoting Bible verses here and there that might fit the narrative. Many churches do not have a constitution or written bylaws yet are called churches. This leadership style has damaged the image of pastoral leadership and creates countless problems in the Anyuwaa congregations. This problem is found across the board from Sunday services to church leadership, and also across the denominations in the Anyuwaa church.

For example, in Mekane Yesus, my former church, we cherish being offshoots of the Presbyterian church. However, now that I serve as a Presbyterian ordained pastor, I see that our leadership system and model are contrary to that of the East Gambella Bethel Mekane Yesus. Taking Ebensburg or Colver Presbyterian churches, my current ministry context, as an example, as in other Presbyterian congregations, the pastor is the moderator of the session, which we called *jø døøk a cööng Jwøk in Dha-Anyuwaa*. The pastor moderates meetings and oversees the overall activities of the church while elders and deacons carry out crucial and respective specific tasks. The pastor leads, preaches, and teaches as well as visits those with spiritual needs.

That is not the case in Mekane Yesus of Gambella. In Mekane Yesus, for example, while there might be seven or nine elders on the session or the congregation council or ቤተ ክርስቲያን ሽማግሌ, in Amharic, the pastor appears at the meetings as an observer. He/she gives suggestions but does not moderate the meeting. The chairperson of the elders, which in our Presbyterian leadership would be the clerk of the session, is the moderator of the council and has a stronger voice than the other elders and congregation. The council leader assigns preachers, creates agendas, and is the sole head of the congregation.

The East Gambella Bethel Synod in particular is a mix of Lutheranism, due to its ties to the national church, the Ethiopian Evangelical Church Mekane Yesus, and the Presbyterian Church because of the founding missionaries. While the church is doctrinally immersed in Lutheranism as mentioned above, structurally, it should have followed a Calvinistic leadership style as the church now follows Calvinistic leadership. However, this model of leadership is neither of Lutheran nor Presbyterian. Even in the Lutheran church, the pastor is the ex officio president of the congregation and the congregational council and has similar responsibilities as in the PCUSA. Therefore, the East Gambella Mekane Yesus seems to be lost in the middle of two denominations or has simply adapted to its own style which must have emerged from the government leadership style.

This sounds like a servitude leadership style and does not reflect the servanthood type. And it was the reason that in 2007 I wrote my thesis for my bachelor of biblical theology on a similar topic. My title then was about the destiny of pastors and pastoral ministry in the Ethiopian Evangelical Mekane Yesus (EECMY). My research was conducted in seventeen of the twenty synods of that church. And the study seamlessly showed that pastors were sidelined, paid poorly, served part-time, and in most cases served voluntarily, yet were required to do more than they ought to. It pleases me now that the EECMY has proposed a minimum payment for pastors nationwide and is recommending some changes in leadership. However, the church in Gambella is still tied to the old system, and the Anyuwaa church in general remains in the grip of a leadership crisis, a lack of discipleship ministry, a proliferation of false teachings, and the continued threat of customs and traditions that run counter to gospel values.

Sadly, many Anyuwaa churches have followed this type of leadership because many of them departed from the East Gambella Mekane Yesus, and this crisis affects the whole church irrespective of denomination. Could this leadership model invite discrepancies, and might it be the reason the church lacks a discipleship approach and invites disputes and church divisions in the Anyuwaa church? Certainly. The lack of an applicable discipleship model and failure in leadership systems can be traced to this church practice, where pastors are barred from taking full responsibility for church leadership. Ordained pastors are wrestling with how to shepherd their flocks. Evangelists and prophets are being assigned to the Sunday services and pastors are being allowed to preach only once a month, with luck. Unfortunately, lack of leadership and biblical education background for those elected for leadership adds to this agony. Regardless of circumstances, the church must know that "pastors have the task of preaching the gospel and administering the sacraments, and in so doing they are connected with a particular congregation."[8]

John Calvin is right. The main task of the pastor is teaching and proclaiming the word in preaching. Therefore, as in the other local Ethiopian churches and in the Americas, the church of the Anyuwaa should acknowledge this main task of pastors and provide the opportunity for them to lead, preach, and teach while being supported by the committee members and the church at large. That is the profit and advantage of partnership. In doing so, *the Anyuwaa church will avoid the intrusion of self-ordained pastors, prophets, and apostles, and stand firm in the teachings of Scriptures and biblical principles and shape the church of Christ in the Anyuwaa land* (2 Thess 2:15). And to foster a working model of leadership or discipleship, the Anyuwaa church needs to understand that, in leadership, we are unpacking our brokenness, imparting gifts, and inspiring and encouraging our followers as well as challenging ourselves.

Therefore, in the light of partnership, the Anyuwaa Evangelical Churches Unity (AECU) is the best candidate. This council that holds most of the churches and denominations in Gambella must strive to create a conducive platform for engagement and critically monitoring church practices in Gambella. It must challenge pastors to stand firm in their responses to claims from prophets and traditional practices. It must also be a fundamental truth to hold that while some offices described in Eph 4 are timeless, prophets and apostles are outdated.[9] We must define those terms and offices and what they mean to us today, which I will leave for the reader. We must encourage those calling themselves prophets to be seers because they are not prophesying in the contemporary setting. Likewise, we must encourage those calling

8. Selderhuis, *Calvin Handbook*, 330.
9. Selderhuis, *Calvin Handbook*, 329.

themselves apostles to be disciples as they, too, continue to be learners and imitators of Jesus Christ.

How blessed must it be when the local churches are encouraged to partner and learn from one another? The Anyuwaa Council of Churches must move beyond joint worship to join in a partnership where church challenges are discussed, solutions proposed, and faith enriched concretely. Broadly, each denomination needs to learn the leadership model and system embraced by its denominational branch, then incorporate elements from the Anyuwaa traditional leadership system and maintain a convincing voice and leadership aspiration to the pastor or *Qes*. This means those with a Reformed background must take steps to contextualize Reformed theology and utilize their leadership model to foster growth and maturity. The Baptists, the Lutherans, and nondenominational churches must do likewise.

For example, the Bethesda Evangelical Reform Church could partner with the church in Gambella or with my current ministry context of Ebensburg and Colver Presbyterian Churches. Both could benefit from this mutual partnership as they continue to learn from one another. The Bethesda Evangelical Reform Church could utilize the leadership approach where the pastor is the moderator and committees are chaired by separate members and serve as models. The Ebensburg and Colver, on the other hand, could also learn from the outreach models of the Bethesda Church, where members engage in group home visitation. Occasional gatherings and coffee time can also be utilized in our American context. This is where a member makes coffee and invites neighbors. Yet, the Ebensburg and Colver churches can substitute coffee with something else that helps invite our neighbors.

Despite the individualistic culture of America, we might, with prayer and discernment, explore the possibility of encouraging members of the congregations to reach out to others by sponsoring informal neighborhood gatherings, extending friendship and fellowship to lonely or introverted members of the community. We might also learn and adapt to a worship style where praise songs are sung and we start moving in dance and joyfully ascribing to God his wondrous acts of love. Bethesda may learn from the enrichment days of our presbytery where a day or two are set aside and members learn about different topics, pray, and share fellowship time outside of regularly scheduled worship times. May we share our diverse spiritual gifts and strengthen our faith for divine purposes.

4. *Exhortation in Discipleship*

While a few study group members indicated discipling their members, the majority seem to have adopted a hands-off approach and have abstained from action for fear of losing members who might become angry if challenged. However, this perception and action is contrary to the biblical essentials of preaching the gospel of truth. "How can we stop speaking of what we have learned, seen, and heard?" Peter asked boldly (Acts 4:20; 2 Cor 5:19–20). Church leaders and pastors must be aware that they are commissioned and committed to the task of reconciliation, and that includes exhortation. We must understand the church and its purpose. Because of its biblical and ecclesiastical foundation, as John Calvin perceived, "The church is elected by God to serve as a tool of God and to make community with Christ possible and real."[10] The church has the power to bind and untie for the sake of the gospel proclamation (Matt 18:18).

In whatever circumstances, it is also unwise to regard or mistake exhortation with punishment. The purpose of exhortation or discipline in our contemporary language is to maintain the unity and purity of the church as we love one another and put others ahead of oneself. It is advice, encouragement, and an entreaty by the church of Christ and a close follow up to bring a member back to the right path of faith. It is to correct irregularities and delinquencies in the church of Christ. Paul exhorted Eudia and Syntyche to live in harmony with the Lord and one another (Eph 4:2; 5:1–2; Phil 2:1–30). This principle has been passed through centuries of the Christian church, and we are called to obey it.

10. Selderhuis, *Calvin Handbook*, 323.

In principle, if an individual persists in disruption of the church, such a person does not belong to the church or the respective denomination. He or she must be released, but it must be done in accordance with the bylaws and procedures of discipline of the respective church and with love (1 Cor 5:12–13). Yet, the problem in the Anyuwaa church, as mentioned earlier, is the lack of bylaws and disciplinary procedures to follow when investigating or making decisions on matters of discipline. As a result, many agree that when individuals are discipled and disciplined, they often take such actions as punishment to bar them from their respective ministries. However, the Anyuwaa church must act and create formal leadership models to help safeguard the authenticity of leadership for the sake of the church of Christ. Likewise, church members need to be made aware that "knowing God requires cognitive union with him in which our whole being is affected by his love and holiness"[11] (Rom 12:2–3; Eph 4:17–24) that we get rid of our old life as we allow the Holy Spirit to transform us from within, and that includes adapting to the new life in Jesus Christ and abiding by the principles of the church.

The church needs to define and redefine its ethos and transform its identity through small group Bible reflections, group prayer, and occasional retreats for pastors and church leaders. The Anyuwaa Council of Churches can take the leadership and denominations can contribute to such initiatives. The church must reflect on the virtues of Christ's life. Imitating Christ cannot be achieved without spiritual maturity, and without a deep understanding and persistent application of the virtues of Scripture. Virtue is truth, distilled and applied to the individual life. All we know, all we understand, all we believe about the truths of the Bible must come together into patterns of thinking and attitude, and should be pursued with words and our deeds as well.

We are called to be in the middle ground morally, ethically, religiously, and practically as we lead our lives in Christian faith of our era. Like the old Israel, we are called to give up the ways of Egypt (which represent our traditions, old selves, and way of

---

11. Osmer, *Teaching Ministry*, 17.

life). We must not act like the Canaanites or adopt their practices (sorcery, divination, and bewitchment). We must live as people who have departed yet are still in the middle of their journey—the "now" and "then" before Christ returns. Christ himself has called us out to demonstrate our new birth in him and live like a shining light on hillside. As a light lit on a hillside cannot be hidden from views, and as salt draws many to its taste, so too is our Christian living in this world. We cannot hide our faith from others if we truly abide in the teachings of Christ. And when we live out our faith as Jesus demands of us, Jesus said we are then giving God the glory and praises he deserves (Matt 5:13–16; Exod 22:18).

In conclusion, as Paul exhorted the Corinthians and the Thessalonians, may we also continue to confront immorality such as polygamy and other bad practices. May we warn the disruptive, encourage the disheartened, help the weak, and be patient toward others. May we strive to do what is good for everyone. May sincerity and truth be at the core of our endeavor in encouraging competent and faithful discipleship (1 Thess 5:13–16; 1 Cor 5:1–8).

5. Enlightening Prayer

What can we do without prayer in church? Prayer is the only means by which we ask God to supply our needs, to strengthen our faith and our relationships, and to grant us wisdom to proceed in our plans in ministries and family lives. Prayer is the most effective way or action to take to bring desired outcomes of discipleship and faith formation. Jesus prayed for his ministry, encouraged us to pray, and will grant our request. Paul, the most powerful man in the New Testament, partnered with others in prayer and asked churches to pray for him. Paul knew the power of prayer, that through prayer the Lord opened his mind, endowed him with knowledge, encouraged him to speak boldly, and then revealed the mystery of the gospel for which he was called to be an ambassador known to many (Eph 6:18–20). He knew he could not do anything without prayer and to the Ephesians he wrote and said, "I pray that the eyes of your heart may be enlightened in order that you may know the hope to which he has called you, the riches of his glorious inheritance in his holy people" (Eph 6:18–20 NIV).

The study showed that while the church participated in joint worship and conducted countless spiritual conferences throughout the year, prayer for discipleship ministry or for radical changes in the church was not mentioned in the discussion nor in the interviews. Anything we do must be led by enlightening prayer. *An enlightening prayer is a prayer by which we intentionally and consciously pray and believe that the merciful God opens the gates of the heavens and will grant us our request.* This book project has been drenched and saturated with prayer. I have been asking individuals to pray since the beginning of this project in 2018. Through clouds of challenges, the Lord lined up people to assist in proofreading and providing resources for the project. In prayer we break barriers, tear down towers, and demolish stone walls of procrastination. As a result, we celebrate and give God the glory.

We must know that the problems of idleness, the lack of a discipleship approach that fosters Christian maturity, and the challenges of tradition are all magnified because the church does not prioritize prayer. Scriptures tell us how the devil lurks and roars like a lion to devour and divide (1 Pet 5:8). Our African lions lie patiently as they follow a herd of buffalo until they single out the weak and lonely. Only when we pray can we remain sober-minded and alert to keep the adversaries at bay. When we engage in conscious prayer, we grow, help others foster their faith, and are empowered. It is unfortunate for the church and pastors of the Anyuwaa for not partnering in prayer. When we pray, we can speak truth of the gospel, teach principles, and engage in decent relationships with others. When we devote ourselves to enlightening prayer, the Holy Spirit takes leadership, keeps us alert, and guides us in our discernments. May we pray that the eyes of our understanding are enlightened and that we are capable of knowing what God holds for us. For it is when we pray that we continue in the word and become true disciples (John 8:30–31).

6. *Discernment*

Discernment is the process by which a church realizes its limitations and depends on God's grace. In that, the church looks at the past, present, and future and sees what is useful for itself. It is a methodology and a pattern by which church leaders teach "congregations how to understand the circumstances of their everyday life and world in terms of God's promises future," and the church must discern where it is going.[12]

The Anyuwaa church is in such state at this moment. Taking this into account, discernment is the major challenge for the Anyuwaa church. It seems the church dug a hole for itself as it failed to teach and orient members, yet wrestled with day-to-day activity without discerning, making plans, and exploring better approaches. This may be a time for this church to look at a rescuing effort, in that God may bring a helper. It is time for the Anyuwaa church to "test the spirits in order to distinguish between the seductive spirits of the old age and the Spirit of new creation."[13]

Failing to view things through the lens of the gospel always leads us to the blindness of syncretism, and we are buried in an endless pit, where bad practices are carried out in the church of Christ. May we view our current challenges with the hope of resurrection and the restoration of church norms and practices. The church can shape its identity through faith formation and group Bible studies to help discern the mystery of God in their present state. Discerning the Spirit of God reassures the church and reminds the believing community of the covenant, the promise of God, and provides hope for their future.

Suggestions for the Church

This project study could be done over a broader spectrum. This one is concerned only with the pastors and churches in Gambella, Ethiopia, and a few pastors in the Americas. Although there are

12. Osmer, *Teaching Ministry*, 27.

13. Osmer, *Teaching Ministry*, 44.

limited published materials on this specific matter, this study could be replicated, and a study could be done with both churches of the Anyuwaa in South Sudan and those in the refugee camps. The study could also be narrowed down by taking one church from Gambella, Ethiopia, and one in Pochalla or Juba, South Sudan, as models for study. I am convinced that we will be rewarded with informative results. It will be interesting to see how the discipleship ministry is carried out in the Anyuwaa church of South Sudan or the Anyuwaa emerging churches in the refugee camps in Kenya.

I would suggest Richard Robert Osmer, *The Teaching Ministry of Congregations*, and *The Radical Disciple* by John Stott to be the leading references in such a study or any teaching ministry or leadership and discipleship trainings. Some of the suggestions such as "The Anyuwaa Traditional Religion and the Bible Preacher," a thesis by Ojod Miru Ojulu, as well as *African Spirituality: Forms, Meanings and Expressions*, from World Spirituality and edited by Jacob K. Olupona, can also be utilized to understand the Anyuwaa traditional religion background and challenges to the church.

Lastly, based on the suggestions in this context study, it would be possible to replicate this study with extensive interviews, focus group discussions, and surveys when and where it is permissible. It would be encouraging to conduct extensive interviews with those renowned figures, a blend of older and younger pastors in the church of the Anyuwaa. When the study is conducted with the intent to present a practical discipleship approach and the importance of teaching ministry in the church, we will be encouraged to move as a church that is called to do the will of God among the Anyuwaa people and earth. And only when we engage in practical discipleship will the church be infinite miles wide in mission intervention and infinite miles deep in faith growth. As Don William McClure witnessed years past, may a new generation of Anyuwaa Christian believers be born in our twenty-first century in this new kingdom of Jesus Christ.[14]

14. Partee, *Story of Don McClure*, 253–54.

CHAPTER 6

Conclusion and Summary

Teach and Make Disciples

THROUGHOUT THIS STUDY AND assessment, we have embraced the essence, purpose, and goal of discipleship and the truth of our calling to live as disciples. A true disciple, Jesus said, is like the owner of a house who brings from the storeroom new treasure as well as old (Matt 13:52). This is the goal of discipleship: to be grounded in the truth of Scriptures, live in the Word, and put forth such truth as we serve others and make Christ known to the world. Discipleship originated from God; thus, as we share the gospel message, we act and exert that gift as we minister to others, continue living in his word, and drink from the fountain of the Holy Spirit to strengthen us in our journey of faith in this world.

Therefore, with this assessment and study, we can now conclude that there is little understanding of discipleship ministry and approach in the Anyuwaa church for the work that Jesus called and commissioned the church and community of believers to accomplish—teach and make disciples (Matt 28:18–20).

In summary, we learned that there was little opportunity or resources for the Anyuwaa church to develop biblical understandings of discipleship since the coming of missionaries to the Anyuwaa land. Due to challenges presented by the government of Ethiopia in prohibition of the use of Latin alphabet, the whole Bible was not translated until 2010, after more than sixty years of missionaries coming to the Anyuwaa people. As a result, the Anyuwaa church experienced setbacks in terms of biblical and theological understandings of the Christian faith. We learned that the changes had existed even at the turn of the decade and during the regime change in Ethiopia, that the gospel was preached but not much attention was given to teaching the basic principles of the Bible, and that discipleship was not at the core of those movements. This is because of the lack of teachers and leaders with biblical knowledge since there were minimal theological education opportunities for many leaders and evangelists. We can attribute the church growth to their diligence and tireless endeavors. Yet, although church membership grew quickly, many members did not develop a mature understanding of the expectations of that membership. Membership growth outstripped growth in maturity. Over time, the Anyuwaa church became more and more unstable and lacked foundation. As a result, our study showed that the Anyuwaa have formed an unsettled church when it comes to theology, doctrine, and church leadership and that much work still needs to be done. A biblical disciple approach that aims to incorporate local resources and embed them into the gospel teaching is deemed best to shape and align the church with biblical principles for our faith.

As a result of lacking trained Bible teachers and preachers and a strong discipleship approach, leadership and polygamy have been persisting challenges to the Anyuwaa church and have brought division, dropouts, and weakness to the authenticity of biblical principles of marriage and leadership. The threat of witch doctors, traditional gods and superstition, and lack of partnership between the churches are part of the equation. Likewise, unsuccessful mitigation of movements of the Murle tribe and the influx of the Nuers from South Sudan and constant tribal clashes have been part of the problem. There have been expansions, abduction of children, and aggression since the regime change of 1991. Since then, western Anyuwaa territory on the bank of the

Opëënö River, part of Jöör, Cïrö and Nyikaani, has been deserted due to the instability, and the gospel movement in these areas was aborted for nearly thirty years. This has brought mounting pressure on the Anyuwaa church and the inability to evangelize and plant churches in those areas.

Therefore, this study project presents considerable implications for the Anyuwaa church, where an applicable discipleship approach is lacking. It is true, as the study has shown, that the Anyuwaa people are religious, and their worldview includes strong belief in spiritual matters. They have distinct views regarding spiritual realms and physical matters. Their customary practices exhibit a keen awareness of the essence of life in its present state and beyond the physical sphere.

However, much is lacking when it comes to preaching and teaching gospel narratives through the lens of Anyuwaa culture. Such an interpretation of the gospel message would allow a balanced preaching of the gospel as related to the paradigm of our culture. The church must seriously consider ecclesiological catechesis as an important step in the aspect of faith that requires distinctive discerning action to bring changes in the church and in the life of a Christian person. We must follow the tradition and practice of the ancient church in allowing people to the church of Christ. The church must not, as in the words of William Barclay, allow any person "into the Christian Church on a moment of emotion."[1] People need to be instructed, made known their responsibility and what Christ demand for their faith journey in the church.

The Anyuwaa church must start a catechesis curriculum in variety of formats not only to prepare members for membership or confirmation, but also to build investment and trust in the gospel, convert followers, and transform them into leaders who desire to do the will of their Lord. It is when we start catechizing that we begin to empower people and build up interest in continued learning that leads to discipleship and faith growth. As we begin such programs, we must also seek trained leaders. *A theologically educated leader is an informed partner in the mission and*

1. Barclay, *Letter to the Romans*, 91.

preaching of the gospel. This is not to minimize the lay leadership, but to state the fact and the need for theological education in the Anyuwaa church. Study shows that many leaders, evangelists, and prophets lack theological education and, therefore, the present discipleship problem is linked to such privation.

Thus, contextualization of the gospel message is an essential step in the discipleship approach. This is a call for the church to start interpreting the gospel message utilizing contextual elements of our culture and interpret them through the lens of the gospel message. When we do so, this study proves that the church will avoid syncretism and the pressure from traditions that tend to mislead faithful believers. For example, prayer and healing play a vital role in the Anyuwaa cultural practice. The Anyuwaa people believe in the power of spoken words, that words bring healing and restore the right of health and well-being perverted by sickness, infertility, and misfortune. Healing is accomplished primarily through words of prayer. They have practice in chasing away bad spirits invading human territory. They believe that words have the power to repel curses, to pronounce blessings, and to heal sickness. Therefore, when we start interpreting such strong beliefs within the truth of the gospel, it is proof that we have come to the best discipleship approach—bringing new as well as old treasures to light as we speak the truth and the fulfillment of the gospel in the life of our church and the hearts of our believers.

As we aim to develop a practical discipleship model that fosters spiritual maturity in the Anyuwaa church, it is vital to hold on to and maintain biblical partnership and practice discipline. When we devote ourselves to strengthening our faith, we become strong and share gifts among us and within the system. As leaders we need to allow ourselves to accept exhortation as we exhort others. In doing so, we will allow others to see exhortation as a healthy practice for the well-being of the believing community and the sanctity of the church.

A Call toward Contextualizing the Gospel Message

As Christians we are called to imitate Christ and are invited to reflect on the virtues of Christ's life. We are challenged to live as we are called and be holy as our Father and do the will of him, who has called us to faith (1 Cor 7:17; 1 Pet 1:16–18; John 5:19). We are challenged to reject conformity but are invited to allow ourselves to be transformed. Yet, we cannot attain such virtues without spiritual maturity and without a deep understanding and persistent application of such virtues. However, we must know that no one attained Christ's life by his or her own strength and mental ability, but through sanctification. And sanctification is the process of transformation and the course of renewal from within through the power of the Holy Spirit. When we submit to the will of God and allow ourselves to be transformed by the Holy Spirit, we will indeed begin renewing our minds and soften our hearts so that we are able discern what is good, pleasing, and the perfect will of God (Rom 12:2). Because discipleship is indeed a process of transformation of oneself, it is a call to encounter culture and reflect the will of Christ in the way of life and faith.

The Anyuwaa church is now called to challenge the culture of syncretism and fear of witch doctors, to bring a culture of solidarity and firm belief in the truth of the gospel, and to contextualize the gospel message. We can change the old method and create a new approach as we allow ourselves to learn and interpret the gospel in the paradigm of our culture and worldview. We can do that when we understand the importance of discipleship and teachings as means by which we preserve the truth of the gospel. Because, as John Calvin has said, "the church of God will never preserve itself without a Catechism, for it is like the seed to keep the good grain from dying out, and causing it to multiply from age to age."[2]

We must, therefore, conclude with what Jesus has said of a true disciple, that "if you continue in my word, you really are my disciples. You will know the truth, and the truth will set you free" (John 8:31–32 RSV). Jesus challenges us to live in the word and

2. Selderhuis, *Calvin Handbook*, 206.

continue living out the truth so that we claim our allegiance to Christ and joyfully live as disciples who have been set free from norms and fears but maintain the truth of Christ who has the word and life and reflects true discipleship. We are called to grow in the will of God; called to fellowship with others; to worship God only; called to witness the gospel of salvation to others; called to discipline ourselves, to live holy as God intends for us; and called to claim citizenship in God's realm and heavenly kingdom (Eph 1:18–19; 1 Pet 2:19).[3] We must learn and live as we are called to this truth. Lastly, but not least, may we dedicate ourselves to prayer for the spiritual insight that the Lord God enlighten our perceptions, the discernment of our hearts, and the understanding of our minds that we are able to know the hope of his calling, the richness of his gifts, the immeasurable greatness of his power, and his will of inclusion in God's own family.

May the Lord Jehovah grant us this we ask of him. Amen!

3. Stott, *Radical Disciple*, 97–98.

Appendix I: Questionnaires

DISCUSSION QUESTIONS:

January 29, 2020

I HAVE HAD THIS question lingering in my mind for many years. Many of you pastors, elders, evangelists, and faithful believers are aware of how Christianity came to our area through missionaries. In the early years of 1980s EC/1990s, with the regime change in Ethiopia, the word of God spread remarkably. By year 1994, many villages were touched by the gospel movement as far as Jor and across the border of South Sudan. New ways of worship were formulated, speaking in tongues were introduced, and ministry of healing was extremely pursued.

As a result, the Anyuwaa embraced denominational bindings but without clear doctrinal and liturgical differences. However, why the Anyuwaa church lacks foundation and spiritual growth when it comes to Christian life remains unanswered question. These preliminary research questions are for my doctorate program. I decided to explore and to understand the cause better and in return I would present my findings and be a resource for discipleship trainings or for personal use.

Thank you in advance. I value your time and appreciate your help to make this research possible.

Here are my questions and I hope you are able to understand these questions and reflect on them sincerely and truthfully.

1. What do you think is the reason members switch churches or give up faith in the Anyuwaa church?

2. Do you think there are Christians who still be afraid of being bewitched? Or seek counsel from witch doctors? Do we have such people in our Diaspora community?

3. Do you think there are still Christians who fear or believe in a curses from an elder or believe in village gods?

4. Polygamy is highly practiced among devoted Christians, including leaders in the Anyuwaa church. Why and what do you think might be the reason? In which ways or areas do you see our tradition is affecting the Anyuwaa church or reasons you see our tradition is affecting our church, both negatively and positively?

5. Where have you seen or do you see growth in the faithful living among the members of your specific church?

6. What do you think might be a solution for these issues affecting our churches?

የምርምር ጥያቄዎች:- ጥር 29 ቀን 2020

ይህ ጥያቄ ለብዙ ዓመታት በአእምሮዬ ውስጥ ሲመላለስ ቆይትዋል :: ብዙዎቻችሁ ፓስተሮች ፣ ሽማግሌዎች ፣ የወንጌል ሰባኪዎች እና ታማኝ አማኞች ክርስትና በሚስቶኖች እንዴት ወደ አካባቢያችን እንደመጣ ታዉቃላችሁ :: እ.ኤ.አ. በ 1980 ዎች / 1990 ዎች የመጀመሪያ ዓመታት በኢትዮጵያ ውስጥ የአገዘዝ ለውጥ ሲመጣ የእግዚአብሔር ቃል በአስደናቂ ሁኔታ በአካባቢያችን ተሰራጨ :: እስከ 1994 ድረስ ብዙ ሠፍራዎች እስከ ጆር እና ከደቡብ ሱዳን ድንበር ባሻገር በወንዙሉ እንቅስቃሴ ተነኩ :: አዲስ የአምልኮ መንገዶች ተቀርፀዋል

፤ በልሳኖች መናገር ተጀምሯል ፤ እና የመረወስ አገልግሎትም እጅግ በጣም ተከታትሏል ::

በእነዚህ ዓመታት የአኙዋ በተ ክርስቲያን የሃይማኖት መግለጫዎችን ያለ ግልጽ አስተምህሮ እና ሥነ-መለኮታዊ ልየነቶች ተቀብሏል:: ጥያቄው ግን ወደ እምነት በሚመጣበት ጊዜ ለምን መሠረት ወይም እድገት የማያሳየዉ ለምንድን ነዉ? እነዚህ የምርምር ጥያቄዎች ለዶክትሬት መርሃግብሬ ናቸዉ ::

የእነዚህ ተግዳሮቶች መንስኤ ምን እንደሆነ ለመዳሰስ እና ለመረዳት ወሰንኩ :: በመጨረሻም ፤ ለደቀመዝሙርነት ስልጠናዎች ሊያገለግል የሚችል መረጃ እና ሰነድ አቀርባለሁ : ፤ የቀደም ምስጋና አቅርብልቆታለዉ:: ይህንን ምርምር እዉን ለማድረግ ጊዜዎን ሰለስጡ እናም እገዛዎን አደንቃለሁ ::

ጥያቄዎቹ እንደሚቀጠሉ ናቸዉ፤ እንደሚሩትም ተስፋ አደርጋለሁ ::

1. አባላት ቤተክርስቲያናትን የሚቀይሩበት ወይም እምነትን የሚተዉበት ምክንያት ምን ይመስልዎታል?

2. ጥንቆላ የሚፈሩ ክርስቲያኖች አሉ ብለዉ ያስባሉ? ወይም ከጠንቋዮች ምክር የሚይዙ ይኖር ይሁን?

3. አሁንም እርግማን የሚፈሩ ወይም እርግማን የሚያምኑ ወይም በመንደር ሐማልክት የሚያምኑ አሉ ብለዉ ያስባሉ?

4. ከአንድ በላይ ማግባት በቤተክርስቲያኖቻችን ውስጥ እና በታማኝ ክርስቲያኖች ዘንድ በጣም ይተገበራል :: ለምን እና ምን ሊሆን ይችላል ብለዉ ያስባሉ? ወጋችን በየትኞቹ መንገዶች ወይም አካባቢዎች በቤተክርስቲያናችን ላይ ተጽዕኖ እያሳደረ እንደሆነ ታያላችሁ?

5. በአባላትዉ መካከል በታማኝነት የመኖር እድገትን የት ተመልክተዋል?

6. በቤተክርስቲያናችን ላይ ለሚከሰቱት እነዚህ ጉዳዮች መፍትሄዉ ምን ሊሆን ይችላል ብለዉ ያስባሉ?

Appendix II: Verbatim Interview Notes

FOCUS GROUP VERBATIM

June 10, 2021

Gambella, Ethiopia

Background

This group discussion was aimed to investigate the overall aspects of the challenges of discipleship ministry and the effect of tradition and divinities that are affecting the life of the Anyuwaa church. And also it is to explore the level of the pastors' knowledge concerning such issues.

As such, the research project was conducted based on a hermeneutic phenomenological method with strong elements of ethnographical aspects. It seeks to show the source of the current discipleship crisis and encourages continued discussion to present a practical and effective discipleship approach for the Anyuwaa church.

Plan

While there were constant informal conversations regarding the focus group discussion, the meeting with pastors was planned for June 10, 2021, at 5:00 p.m. in Gambella, Ethiopia. This discussion has two formats and in the following transcriptions both formats are demonstrated. First, the discussion began using a "going-around-the-table" format. Individuals around the table are encouraged to contribute, replying to the question following the order in which they are seated. Second was a "popcorn" format. This approach gives individuals freedom and motivates them to contribute as they felt moved.

Observation

Two pastors arrived at Giwa Hotel early. That to me indicated the level of interest for discussion. Only ten minutes into the hour, the meeting already started. That does not pertain to African practice or respect for time. As everyone was seated around the table, the discussion began with an introductory statement, and the rest of our time was full of energy as we were served fresh drinks. We celebrated afterward by way of saying "thank you" to the pastors for their time and sharing their knowledge during this group discussion.

Verbatim Reflections and Transcriptions

In the transcription or paraphrasing of the conversation, the names are transcribed using three letters for the purpose of confidentiality: "P" for pastor and "Q" for *Qes* ("the reverend" in Amharic), accompanied with initials. Since most names start with an "O," some of the initials will be changed to avoid similarities. Individual responses will be numbered to indicate the sequence of the conversation and to help guide the reader. "R" will represent my responses as a researcher. However, full names of the informants or focus group discussion members will appear in resource lists at the end.

While everyone was settled, I began and asked pastor GN to open our discussion with the word of prayer.

QGN—1—God our Father, we thank you for gathering us together to talk about your church. Lead us now as we discuss, may good ideas emerge from this meeting for our church. We ask that you open our minds and our hearts through the power of your Holy Spirit. Amen.

R—1—Thank you everyone for agreeing to participate in the group discussion. Also, I want to express my heartfelt thank you to the Sioux Falls Seminary and my advisor for allowing me to conduct my study project on context of the Anyuwaa church. I could have done my project on something else, but the issue of discipleship is prevalent in our church, and I wanted to research the cause and see what can be done to bring about the solution. This is something to start with to open continued discussion and for the new generation of researchers to build on. I must be aware of some issues, but I also needed you, pastors to share what you know in your ministries. Thus, with this focus group I hope we can identify, define, and name issues the Anyuwaa church is facing in our generation and most importantly when it comes to discipleship ministry.

Now we can go around the table to introduce ourselves and which church you are representing and continue with answering the question; please step in when it is your turn to speak, and our first question is: **What might you think must be the reason members switch churches or give up faith?**

POO—1—This question could be divided into two: *First, the reason why members leave churches to a different denomination, and second, it is when a person leaves faith for worldly life.* There are many things that needed to be studied but we are lacking such expertise. This issue is prevalent in our churches regardless of denomination. What I have come to know is that Anyuwaa are easy to give up on something; when/ if they start something they easily give up. They do not persist in pursuing their goals. This is the reason why the church of the Anyuwaa has been failing and not growing in faith. Peoples feeling are stimulated when something new start in the area, maybe a new church. For this reason, many people leave their churches to join the new emerging church. They leave their own denominations without reason or purpose of leaving. Also, and in general, people leave church because of conflicts. When a conflict persists in a church some people leave, hoping to find a better place with less quarrels, which in most cases they ended up not finding the peace they were seeking. I am sure others may contribute to this and I will share again in the discussion.

PPA—1—Thank you so much for this meeting. This issue needs to be studied more, but regarding our question, first is the problem of quest/seeking—*felega*. People are looking for their needs to be met. They leave their own churches in the hope for a better benefit or life in the new emerging churches. That is the first reason why people leave for new churches or move between churches.

R—2—What I am hearing is that this search is linked to personal needs. Is that right?

PPA—2—Yes, because if they do not get or receive something economically that meet their needs from their respective churches, they think that maybe the new church will provide something better that benefit them financially. Also, there is this understanding that members think that the church is simply an open place and are free to do whatever they want to do even if it's unethical. Some of them may say that their current church follows strict rules. Then think that the new church may not follow their rules strictly, therefore, they can run their lives as they want. These are the two reasons I see why members keep moving between churches and even abandon their faith.

QOO—1—In addition to what has been said, I would also say that people leave church or faith due to lack of teachings. There are no faith-based teachings given to members starting from when they come to faith and offered periodically for faith growth. This affects the Anyuwaa church. People come to faith and joint the church without going through catechism. Biblical discipleship approach is not built in the system. Also lack of full-time pastors is a contributing issue. I can say that this cannot be tied to one issue but a comprehensive problem in the Anyuwaa church that left unsolved or tackled for many years. Teaching aimed at faith growth and spiritual formation is not provided, and too, lack of full-time pastors to take the teaching job seriously. Like I said, the problem we are facing are many things combined. Second, the reason people change churches easily, I would say it is because of misunderstanding and lack of cooperation between the churches. People move between churches using the disunity between churches. Also, personal faith and understanding play great role in deserting faith or switching churches. If someone has a good understanding of faith, switching denominations for personal benefit cannot be a question at all. This is a fall of all the Anyuwaa churches and Anyuwaa as a tribe.

PDT—1—As others have said, members want to live in the church with sin. When they are told or disciplined is when they react and switch church. This includes evangelists and lay leaders. When they are wrong, they want to continue with their ministry while disobeying church rules. Lack of teaching and theological education is also a big problem. Many lay leaders and preachers in our churches do not have any theological education background. Many did not go through any biblical leadership training. Many of them preach and are leading churches only because they can read the Bible and interpret it in any way possible. They lack solid biblical foundation and theological knowledge because whenever they are admonished, then they would easily leave the church. Members too, are going from church to church, not because they have problem in their respective denominations, but only because they wanted to see something new. They say, there is no difference "between this one, or the other." Also, why people leave their faith, the answer to this is our culture. Our culture is still strong on our members. Many of them do not see any value or benefit in the church and their participation. Some of them would rather go back to cultural practices than staying in the church. This also can be traced to lack of reading the Bible. Many members are illiterate. So, it is easier for them to leave their faith since they do not understand what they are involved with anyway. As stated earlier, our churches are led by people who do not have biblical trainings. These people cannot teach other because they cannot provide any knowledge to others through teaching. Not only lay leaders, even those who consider themselves as prophets, no one has biblical training. So, they can say something that hurts the other person, due to lack of knowledge to relate a message to another from a biblical perspective.

> QGN—2—Immaturity and lack of faith leads people to abandon or switch churches. Since people are not grounded in biblical knowledge, members leave churches in search for churches with self-proclaimed prophets. They do not believe that the Bible is still a fresh word of God. Such people are spectators. They keep observing the life and faith journey of individuals in the church. When they see a friend leave the church, they too would follow. Also, if there is disagreement between their friends and the church leadership, and if such person leaves, they too would leave. Also, lack of interest in strong biblical teachings is another problem. People want to be praised and given soft sermons. When you give a life changing or sermon on moral or Christian ethics, they do not want to hear it. However, if you have solid faith and grounded biblical knowledge, you will not be objecting to the biblical knowledge and will not follow anyone leaving the church.

R—3—Thanks again for this round of discussion. In this first question, I am hearing the issues such as: lack of teaching, members refusal to be disciplined by church leaders, the influence of our culture keeping members hostage, and interest in following self-proclaimed "prophets" than listening to the word preached. Now we can move on to the next questions and use "popcorn" format. So, indicate to me when you want to step into the conversation and please wait until the person speaking is finished with his point. But before we move on, I need you to add on this: Do the members leaving the church ask for clearance, or a letter of referral?

PDT—2—The paradox here is that congregations need more members. When an individual comes to church, no one dare to ask to discuss the reason they left their previous church or whether they have good standing with the previous congregation. What churches do is receive that person and give them some task or ministry in the church. This individual is not received to church membership properly; neither are received by reaffirmation of faith, nor profess their faith as they are received with referral. Churches do not even do any investigation on such individuals whether they are divorced, polygamist, or has bad reputation with their previous church. These churches or congregations want to show and say, "We have more members, and our doors are open for anyone to join."

PPA—3—In addition to what PDT said, it is true that members leave the church for many reasons to join a different church. But the evilest thing is that there are evangelists who are actively stocking active members of other churches to lure them to their own churches.

QGN—3—The People who are moving between churches, do so stubbornly. Even if the church tries to meet and discuss to resolve issues, they will choose to leave even if the church is interested in writing a certificate of clearance or letter of referral to the church he or she is moving to. For example, we have an incident in our church. We tried to talk to an evangelist. We told him that we are happy to resolve this problem but if you want to leave, we want you to know that you have the right to leave, but we need to send you to your next church formally. That individual refused to even wait for us to write the letter. Evangelists and self-proclaimed prophets have power over most of the members because they believe that churches need their ministry and can play such game as they want. The big problem too, as stated above, the receiving church do not call or send a letter asking for the person they had received. They do not ask to know why the individual had departed from the previous church and or whether he or she is leaving with good intentions. Evangelists do not listen to the leaders because they claim that they are serving freely and say it is their interest to offer their free service. Therefore, they say no one can stop them. So, people are roaming or moving to churches like herds without a leader.

R—4—We have the organization of unity of churches, right? Would that be something the Anyuwaa churches council needs to act on?

POO—2—The bylaw of the Anyuwaa church council prohibited transition between churches without a proper letter or referral. It encourages churches not to receive anyone joining a different denomination without being accompanied by a letter. However, the bylaw has not been implemented and no one or a church attempts to implement it.

R—5—Our next question, as many people talk about witchcrafts, curse, village gods, and bewitchment, ***do you think there are Christians who are afraid of being bewitched? Or seek counsel from witch doctors?***

POD—1—Since we are in Christ, we come to know many things about our faith. However, people are living double minded. They are in faith but still believe and follow things of the tradition. When they seek help, they follow the advice of others and then they seek the counsel of witch doctors.

On the other hand, those with gifts of prophecy, are believed to be like witch doctor. When someone is facing hardships, others may advise or asked the individual whether they had gone to such and such prophet to be seen or enquire a prophecy. People takes prophets like witch doctors who can tell you fortune or supply healing. It is fair to say that people live in this form of life filled with fear and superstition.

QOO—2—OK, what I want to add here, a few years back, I believe that Christians were strong in faith and churches were determined to destroy witchcraft and sorcery in the Anyuwaa society. During that period no one dared to think about witchcraft, let alone an idea about seeking counsel of witchcrafts. However, in these later years, the believe and practice of witch doctors are widely practiced among believers, and mostly among believers living in the cities. There are Christians fearful of bewitchment. Even if I do not have tangible information, I hear many people talking about individuals saying, "Such and such went to a witch doctor." Also, because in the old days people are afraid of witch doctors, now prophets had taken the place of witch doctors and people are afraid of their voices. Now people are afraid that what the prophet said will caused bad fortune to an individual if a person does not cooperate with the prophet. In this regard, people are fearful of prophets like in the old days with witch doctors. No one question their prophecy or challenge them, but everyone submits to their words, even if most of the prophecies are untrue and misleading.

PDT—3—This exactly is true. These days, Christians are afraid of witch doctors, and they practice sorcery. Many times, people go to witch doctors, and mostly women. When a child is sick, with diarrhea or other persisting illness, people advise the mother of the sick child, saying, "This is an Anyuwaa thing" [meaning, it is something that cannot be treated medically]. And if the mother is tired and runs out of options with this prolonged illness of their child, they would then go to a witch doctor. Second, church members also believe in bewitchment or that someone can spell bad luck on them.

For example, I have two sisters-in-law. One of them was told by a prophet that she has been bewitched by the other wife. After she came home from church service, there was a big chaos in the home and that affected the whole family. It was a big quarrel. And I talked to her husband to relate to his wife that in the Bible we read that there cannot be any spell that works on Christians. She must not worry about such a thing and ignore what her prophet had told her. I want to tell you that there are many Christians who are afraid of curses or of being bewitched.

QGN—4—Bewitchment as you just stated, I do not think there are Christian men who believe in such a thing, but mostly women believers. There are two things that lead women to seek healing or consult witch doctor for fortune: first, when their child is sick, and second, when they are in polygamist relationship and are competing for one man. Many Christian men are also wandering between churches and act as prophets. Like in old days with witch doctors, people are encouraged to go to inquire the prophet so that the prophets foretell their future. In your surprise, when these people go consult these prophets, prophets never lack a word to foretell. Many people live in the shadow and chain of self-proclaimed prophets in the Anyuwaa church today.

R—6—What am hearing is that women seek counsel from witch doctors, young men claim themselves as prophets and move between churches, and prophets have replaced Anyuwaa witch doctors, and that people are afraid of the prophets. If this is what we are all seeing, what can we do about the prophets. I know we are going to talk about the solutions in our closing. The next question is about fear and beliefs. ***Do you think there are still Christians who fear or believe in curses or believe in village gods?*** For example, we have our village god called Dwøle, do you think there is still fear of Dwøle or other gods of the villages?

POO—3—Yes, even these days, you will hear a prophet claiming and prophesy saying, "You have a cord or a thread of a curse lingering from your ancestors." But what we know is no string of a curse that could linger behind or follow anyone who believe in God. The Scripture says, "There is no condemnation for those who are in Christ Jesus" (Rom 8:1 NASB). If we know that we believe in the truth of the gospel, there cannot be any concern of any curse following us. And Scripture also says, "Curse is on the house of the wicked." (Prov 3:33 NASB). The righteous find good and favor and those who does evil finds bad thing from God. So only God puts curses or condemns a person, but no one can spell curse on other. However, you can hear a prophet these days who would say, "You are cursed; your curse has come from so and so." This belief of curses is supposed to be diminishing in our society, but since people are hearing such voices from prophets, people are now talking about curse. You can also see some posters or billboard with the writing saying, "curse will be destroyed" when they advertise their events. These are the people who are propagating and inserting fears in believers and society in general. Now people are talking and believing in the existence and effectiveness of spell curses on believers. It is in our midst and widely spreading among us.

> PAO—1—Pastor, this issue, the sources of these problems, is that people are not introduced to a true faith, or the things of faith are not clear to the members. When we see closely, the Scriptures say whoever is in Christ is a new creation and all things become new (2 Cor 5:17). In this regard, there is no curse or power of curse that can have effect on a believing person. People are still believing in such things because the gospel and teachings are lacking in our churches as PDT has said. If people are taught, they will know that there cannot be any effect of any curse on someone. In their services, prophets would also call a name of someone in the service and claimed that their deceased relatives "such and such died with sadness and so had a spell curse on you or the family and that such

curse is still following you." They are still believing in the effect of curses as if Christ did not die and destroy guilt, sin, and curses. Prophets, too, do not confirm in their prophecy that God has destroyed the curse.

R—7—Just as a follow up, it looks like the prophets leave people in suspension and lingering in thoughts. Do they ever, in their messages, also pronounced the cut of the threat of the curse? If not, why trigger and leave people linger in the thought of the message of the curse?

> PAO—2—Yes, they may say they had cut it, but you can see people would still go home to fight each other. If God speaks the message, it must remain between God and the person who has been given the message. If God says the threat of a curse is cut, there should not be any way that people go home and fight over a spell curse. Also, Christian believers interpret and exaggerate things. You can hear believers saying that it is because of spell curse, that my household and my family has a persisting sickness or are poor or that people are dying. But it must be true that if God cut the curse, it is done, destroyed, and nothing believers should be worrying about.

R—8—Let go back and talk a little bit about village gods, are there still people believing in village gods or following superstition of village gods?

> POD—1—When it comes to village gods, it does not seem to have people who are still following such gods or practice it persistently or strongly. Even the idea of other gods such as god of Nuer, *Cööni* [gods of tribes of Nuer and of Majang respectively bordering the Anyuwaa], or village shrines, are no longer practiced widely. It does seem people have come to faith and believe in the almighty God. However, what we see now, is that people are turning to *kunjuure* [some sort of stems of plants that people wear and believed to have power to protect an individual from harm]. At times of war

or conflicts people hope to conjure up and implore or expel bad lacks or harms. That is an indication that there are people who still believe in such things of tradition, and we can also add into suspicion that people are still believing in the village gods as well.

PDT—4—Well, I think we need to be frank/truthful about this. Many people also think that all these bad things happening to the tribe are because of abandoning the old way of the Anyuwaa. There is still belief in the Anyuwaa village gods or being tied in superstitions. Mostly women still speculate that the spread of diseases and sickness is because of problems related to abandoning or because of curses. Men on the other hand buy *kunjuure* from Pelaate tribe [pastoralist natives going around east Africa]. Also, when there is an event in the village, Christians join and are involved in the dance and rituals. Many Christians these days still believe in the beads associated with village gods and tie them on the writs of their children. They believe that if the beads are not supplied the child will be sick. It come to mind that us pastors, sometimes we tend to look on the surface and are not paying attention to what is going on among believers. For example, when my son married, his wife conceived and during pregnancy with their first child, the parent of his wife asked him to supply beads. They also asked for a goat or sheep to be slaughtered as an *Okïri* [meaning atonement or appeasement]. During the ceremony of this rites, the girl would be sprinkled with the blood and the beads tied on her wrist or waist. The belief is that the gods are appeased and do not harm the mother or the unborn child if supplied with these offerings and sacrifices. Then I refused to meet the demand of such request. So, we need to know that many members are practicing such things. You can see in your churches many children have beads as bracelets. Most of those beads are associated with superstitions of old way of life and demands of village gods. They encourage people to supply such things because they believe that the village god would attack and cause sickness to the child.

QGN—5—Yes, that is true. In addition to what has been stated, many believers also practice *Bak*.[1] *Bak* means exchange or shielding the deceased with the blood of an animal. Even when a Christian person died, they still implement *Bak*. During burial, they kill an animal and pour the blood of such animal in the grave and mix the grave's dirt with blood. This is considered an honored burial. Many people still follow this custom. Even if the deceased is a believing person, you can see believers doing this themselves for deceased relatives.

R—9—Does that means church members value animals' blood over that which Jesus poured for us?

QGN—6—Yes, I guess that is what it means for those who practice it while are still believers.

R—10—Our next question is on polygamy. As many of you know I have been serving with you but now have lived in the States for more than ten years. But in my travels to Gambella, I still learn that polygamy is practiced even more widely, including among the devout Christians. ***Why and what do you think might be the reason? In which ways or areas do you see our tradition is affecting our churches both positively and negatively?***

POO—4—What has been affecting the church, and the reason why people are roaming between churches, is the issue of polygamy. When young men going out with multiple young girls in the choir's group and when the church leaders admonish such individual, they take such action as the reason to move to a different church. I heard some people say that marrying many wives is a gift. I heard a preacher saying that

---

1. Whereas *Okïrï* is considered as atonement or appeasement of the gods to calm the gods not to cause harm to individual, *Bak* on the other hand is killing an animal and have the blood poured or mixed with the dirt during burial as a form of cleansing or to take the life of the animal with the human's. It is an act as shedding the blood of animal in the place of a human or washing the individual with the blood of an animal to purify them as they depart human territory.

one blessing or gift that God has given King David is marrying multiple wives. This is affecting our church and we need to move strategically to stop this. What makes it worse is that those polygamies are also interested in leadership. They want to preach, to lead; they demand their requirements be met and their supporters also petition for them saying, "Why you condemn this person only, what about that person?" [Referring to others who might have multiple mistresses but might be given some responsibility in the church.]

QOO—3—This polygamy has caused a leadership challenge in the church. Even those people whom you dedicate time in discipling and cultivate them to grow into leadership, or the church plan to ordain them to be pastors, you will see them doubling mistresses. Then we end up not having people fit for leadership and wait again for the younger generation to choose leaders from among them. Those too, if they are not trained well, they practice polygamy. This is becoming generational and becoming worse over the years. Last time we had a preacher who had engaged in getting a second wife—when he was issued a letter to stop him from serving, he gathered his supporters and demanded that he must be allowed to preach because he is not the only person who has multiple wives. This is not a one church or a problem of one denomination. All the churches are experiencing this problem. We have the Holy Bible, that is the only resource we have in our hands. What happen is that in all the churches, I would say, there is no bylaws and regulations to guide us in our church ministry. Even if there are things that seem clear in the Bible, they are not implemented in the church. If this continues, we will come to the point saying that "this one has only two wives, maybe we can ordain him." This is because things are getting out of hands, and they are doing everything in the church, and it seems we are not controlling them and are marrying more than two wives now.

POO—5—Let me add to that. I have been trying to disciple some youth, and I am working with the fifth person now. I have started training the first person in hope to help him grow in faith. He failed, the second person failed taking second woman, and now I am training the fifth person. You know, as a pastor, for you to be proud of your work and that you have achieved a goal is when you train someone to replace you, and when you are no longer here, he or she take the responsibility of the church. But now we are in a vacuum. The second thing I ought to say, and I assume is something that is spearheading the misleading for taking many women, is the claim that girls or boys must utilize or put in practice their body parts because it was given by God in assumption to be used. There are preachers who preach such misleading information, that if single girls or boys do not utilize their body parts while on earth, that at the end of ages, God will ask those individuals and judge them for remaining single and failing to use their private parts.

R—11—What does that mean? Does it mean God is going to punish single individuals for not getting married in their lifetime?

POO—6—They are twisting the statement that said, "Multiply and filled the world." "How can we multiply?" they asked.

PPA—4—They say, "Because when God created you, he created you for a purpose, if you go back that way [meaning if someone dies without marrying someone], God is going to judge you because your body part was created to put to use here on earth." Pay attention and think carefully. If a preacher shares such information with a young girl or boy, they will not take that lightly, but they will do something. Even unmarried boys, do you think they will spare time? They will act and take such voice as a blessed instruction from God. As POO has said all our churches are going through a similar situation, and it is getting harder by the day and will continue unless we begin doing something to tackle it.

QGN—7—That is right. What brings division in our churches are problems related to this problem of polygamy. When you have this person whom you think will rise to leadership, you will see them marrying multiple wives. We have a young boy, who pastor Owar may know, that we tried to have admonished, but the people rose against us saying, "Why this boy? Even the elders in the higher leadership, some of them are polygamies." Currently, this problem may seem easier but, in the future, it will get harder when we would seek to ordain pastors. In addition, our churches preach loose sermons. On Sunday, Pastor John preached on a Christian living. While in the middle of the sermon, I saw many people leaving the church to avoid listening to the sermon. I assume this is one of the reasons that people move from church to church. They do not want to listen to strong sermons on morality and Christian living nor follow rules of churches. I tell you, in the future we will not have good preachers nor prophets because they are all interested in many women. There is lack of trust between members and pastors, so I recommend that we change our sermons and preach faith strengthening sermons.

PDT—5—This is saddening and it is going to be hard in the Anyuwaa church in the future. A few years ago, we had organized a biblical course, and not many youths participated. I can see that this issue can be linked to lack of fear or dishonoring God. For example, when preachers preach about marriage, the ones responding to the sermon are older women. Young people do not even listen or pay attention to the sermon. Today, when you are a prophet with multiple wives or a pastor with bad reputation, you can plant a nondenominational church and people still follow them joining their churches. When it comes to church leadership, leaders are afraid to take actions on those who break the rules of the church. They are afraid of choirs' members, members of youth leadership, prophets, and evangelists. They are afraid that if they take an action people will leave the church. I think by letting things loose, we are in the position, like Paul said, of "preaching a different gospel" than the gospel of Jesus Christ (Gal 1:9). When we started our church, one of the members has four wives and divorced some, yet he wanted to be ordained with us. He would go talk to our guest who happened to be a white minister and when the minister came, he announced that "the individuals who will be ordained in Gambella are DT and an individual, X." After many objections on his ordination, the X person came to me and said, "You are one of the people still going around in Gambella saying I have many wives, why are you doing this to me?" We were almost close to a fighting. I told him he will not be ordained; person Y will be ordained in your place. We are following Bible principles and I did not write the Bible, I told him. See, many churches are afraid to talk to an individual who has effective ministry in the church, the fear is that he or she will take people away from the church. Then he or she will continue leading a bad lifestyle in the church. Our culture does not condone going out with multiple women outside marriage. But as I can see, it seems we are creating or have created a different culture in the church where these leaders are free to sleep with multiple young women of the church without taking responsibility for their mistakes. Likewise, it seems young women are preferring going to churches that has many young men.

> PAO—2—All of these we are talking about is to safeguard the future of our tribe and the new generation. It helps shape our future. It is good to talk about marriage. In our current context, even if you are a mature Christian, people are still marrying many wives. It is a natural thing that you listen to or learn about something you do not know. But these people know something about marriage. Like pastor GN has said, the younger Christians are looking up to the older ones. Since the older ones have practiced polygamy, they feel that it is just a normal thing to do. This is because when they are told they always point fingers to the higher body of the church. There was one person who had more than five wives, but people still talk about bringing him to ministry in the church. As pastor OO said, we need to talk but with action and continue to train youth. We have the responsibility to safeguard the lives of these young people. We do not need to ease church regulations, because when we do so we are trying to kill our

culture and the new generation. I can recall, that in the past, when you became a Christian, you would be committed to learning "book one, book two, book three" [this is a reference to the old primers prepared by missionaries. It was a selection of short sentences and verses of the Bible to help new believer read and build faith]. But now there is no such a thing in our churches. When a new person come to church and keep coming for about a month, then they will be given a task to do in the church and even on the pulpit before examining such person. Today, if we start talking about purity in Christian life and if we put in practice our bylaws, you will see many people leaving the church. But what else do we need? We would rather remain with one person then acknowledge God than having majority that dishonor or do not follow God rightly. People are like catfish, they distill the water and move to another section with clear waters but disturb it again. For polygamy practice to stop, as I said above, we the pastors need to take the responsibility. The joint service for the Anyuwaa Council of Church need to be organized differently. There must be more sermons on marriage and be preached regularly. I remember one time when pastor Akwata preached on marriage. When people went back to their homes, the rumors emerged that such things about marriage should not be brought to church. By this incident, it indicated to me that the future of our tribe is darkening, and we need to do something now before it is too late. You are doing the research and you will be going back to America [referring to "R"], but we who are staying here need to start doing something and we will continue with this conversation. When you go to most of congregations, there are not young pastors or someone in line to leadership. We need to keep working on the young generation and try to shape their future.

R—12—Thank you for stating that, yes, as I mentioned earlier this study will not remain on paper. I believe, as we are now trying to find the cause, when the research is finally comprised, I hope this work produces elements for continuing conversation on discipleship. We have talked about problems so far, ***but where have you seen growth in faithful living among your members?***

> PDT—6—On the topic of unity from the pulpit. And the Anyuwaa in our church are one. You cannot disrupt them and divide them. Maybe we are weak in drawing people to our church. In participating in the service of the Anyuwaa Council of Churches, members began to learn about Christian unity and people believe that church is one. Members are now instructing and admonishing themselves without any interference from a leader. At one point someone raised about discrimination, all of them raised their voices said, "You should stop that, here we are not from Openo, from, Jor, etc. [referring to Anyuwaa geographical locations] or from anywhere, we are all one!"

QGN—8—Our church is strong in joining hands together and in visiting people. Our members love to support one another and comfort those who are grieving. They collect money or anything needed when they see someone in need. They do not wait for instructions from a leader, but they initiate and then report to the leader what the members are thinking to do. They bring or report the incident or a case to the church leaders when they see someone going through hardships due to necessity or emotional traumas. Then they will organize and put together a plan of support or to pay a visit to such a person. I know, there are weaknesses in human being, and we have been talking about those shortcomings in our churches, but when we come to members looking after another, our members lack no zeal to support one another. This is a big task in our church.

> QOO—4—We see development in our members when it comes to service participation. Our church members are good at worship both on Sunday services and participating in the weekday's programs. We see people coming to events organized by the church. During these meetings, they ask for

prayer requests and pray for peace in the country, in Gambella, for the loved ones and for the unity of churches. This is good in the life of a Christian person and for the church.

POO—7—I can say that in all our churches we see strong participation in worship. Different sermons with different themes are given, and members have understood the ministry and worship God with Sunday offerings. People give. This is because giving has been introduced and has been implemented with intention in our church. Joint services are attended rightly. I am sure if we continue with this trend, we will leave behind many bad things and the challenges we had talked about.

POD—2—I would relate and concur with everyone who have talked before me. It is true that our members and the leadership are good at working together, whether financial, worship, as well as doing anything that involves physical strength. However, we are lacking and lagging in teaching our members with Bible based knowledge. When we planted our church, we plan to implement discipleship training to help people grow in faith. We have learned early on that lack of discipleship trainings and focusing more energy on worships has make Anyuwaa church weaker in faith growth and biblical knowledge. Therefore, I need to advise everyone, in that if we start helping a new member to grow stronger in faith, the best way is to engage them in discipleship. Those who have been given teachings when they come to faith, they will be stronger believers and among them the church will choose leaders and pastors. We would need these kinds of believers for Bible school with the plan that they will be teachers when they return.

R—13—We are about to conclude our discussion. We have talked about faith, people leaving churches, fear of curses, witch doctors, village gods, polygamy, etc. *What do you think might be a solution to these issues affecting our churches?*

PPA—5—We need more teaching than worship. What we are witnessing in the churches is that people tend to have more interest in worship than attending organized teaching sessions. There is difference between teaching and worshiping. And there are different types of teachings. But we need teaching that is biblically based. These days, I heard that there are people going around giving teachings in the churches. However, such teachings are not built on biblical principles and do not help in building solid Christian faith. We need teachings that targets and tackle false teachings. We need biblical teaching to restore the Anyuwaa church. The Anyuwaa church needs to be restored, Pastor R. You know, this is not that church you are familiar with in the years past; the church of Pastor Degu, Pastor Akway, Pastor Okach, etc. It is not that church anymore. It has changed. Therefore, we need to work hard to restore this church of the Anyuwaa.

PDT—7—We need teaching on unity. We are lacking people who can teach about church unity. These days people have begun to ignore preaching about God and Jesus but instead their church's names. I said this because people are lured by the name of prophets. People say, "If your church does not have a prophet, what are you doing in such a place [their current church]?" And sadly, prophets ask for money. In order to allow a person on the pulpit so that the prophet could lay their hand on an individual, prophets or their assistants ask for one hundred Ethiopian birr [birr is the Ethiopian currency], the sale for an anointing oil costs one hundred birr and some kinds of key chain with the prophet's picture inscribed on it also costs one hundred birr. They will not offer prayer on you unless the required amount is paid in cash. These prophets imitate other prophets. In those prophetic services there is no Bible verse read or preaching of the Scriptures. You cannot hear a word of God preached. "They always say, it is your time today, it is your time today, open your heart, and receive your gift, it your season." They only come to sell their things. So, this issue has affected the church of the Anyuwaa. Even if you keep reminding people not to participate in such worships, they do not listen to you. How are we going to teach these people? They were not brought up with teachings because many did not go through catechism. We need an organized teaching in many churches in our area. Our joint worship has helped us. I have a nephew who was not willing to participate in a church that does not associate with his denomination. When he moved to the village and was not attending any church service that belonged to his denomination, he lagged in faith. The unity of our church needs to be defined because even if we are many denominations, we are one in faith as we worship the same God. We need to find good teachers and focus on building strong unity for our churches for people to be aware of those unbiblical nonsenses. We need an organized seminar where we invite members and leaders of every denomination to participate in the seminar and teaching courses. We need to implement such programs or events, otherwise in the years to come, the Anyuwaa church will be worshiping something else than following the God they had believed in. The solution is using this platform and invite our people in the Diaspora to come and with friends; come and teach us. Yes, we are strong in unity in our church, like mentioned above, but when it comes to prophets, our members' ears itch to listen and all attend services that involve prophecies. We have people who dedicated to teaching healthy marriage, but young women do not want to participate, rather they want to be in churches that have young men who simply sleep with girls. The solution is giving training with deep meaning. Even if those leaders are against training, we can have their respective churches participate in the training or seminar and then they can take the message back to them.

> POO—8—Keeping the purity of the church is the responsibility of the pastors. Eli's family was destroyed because of impurity and mismanagement. In our church, a person who is polygamous is not allowed to teach or lead. That also become a factor and many people left our church. Church is belonged to God; people do not own it. We would rather stay with fifty people in our church than a thousand people that

do not follow the rule of the church. Those in evangelism and mission positions need to act on that. We are responsible for the work of God. We should not be afraid of our members. Let us use the Bible as a reference. For example, we have three people we had placed under discipline. We gave them three to six months for correction. But they refused to comply. This suspension was only served for correction. The plan was that after the period given to them, those individuals would be allowed to resume their leadership. Therefore, we do not allow people to practice what they want and defile the church like Eli. Let us not be afraid of people but practice God's words.

QOO—5—I want to add on what pastor OO had said. We need rules and regulations in the church because in that we have statements or rules on discipline. When we need to discipline someone, we would only refer to such rules and articles. Each church must have such documents to guide them. We also need AECU (Anyuwaa Evangelical Churches Unity) to be strong. Since churches want participation and inclusion in this agency, we can make this office stronger so that AECU spread the message. Use AECU as a medium to convey and dispense messages. Also, teachings of each church, meaning the doctrine of each denomination need to be followed. I can see that we are all failing in one way or another. People are saying that all the churches in Gambella are "Mekane Yesus," except for Anglican. This is because almost all churches in Gambella follow leadership style and similar things like Mekane Yesus does [this is because nearly have of the churches in Gambella have their root in the Mekane Yesus as it was the first church in Gambella, and many churches stem out of it]. Only the Anglican has separate liturgy. Therefore, we need churches to have their own liturgy. Something we need to know, in the church, we have unity in diversity. Since many people think churches are all the same, we need to help them understand and know the difference between our denominations. We need to implement marriage teaching, not in a sermon but a teaching style. We must have something in place to start teaching believers from their conversion. I am sure if we implement all of these we will come up with the solution and solve the problem that we are facing right now.

R—14—Are there any people coming to you for marriage counseling? You have been mentioning the need for teaching. Do you think there must be people assigned to take teaching as their tasks in the churches? Since we are running out of time and I do not want to take your time, please notify me through email or Facebook messenger if you have any questions or anything you want to share and need to be included in our discussion.

POO—9—One thing I wanted to add before our conclusion is some advice. Please talk to people. Talk to your members; send leaders to Bible school, using a plain Holy Bible may help or it may be important, but without biblical education, this Bible becomes a chemistry, a physics, a geography, and can turn into something else. The church is falling and failing. This is the solution. I am a witness. We had one member who was out of hand, but when he went to Bible school, he came back knowledgeable, calm, and able to preach sermons based on biblical knowledge.

R—15—I concur with what you just said that we continue to talk to people and not to be afraid of losing members.

Our group discussion concluded with word of prayer: "Thank you, God, and we are giving you glory for giving us this time. Time is yours but you gave us this short one. You had planned a long time ago that we will meet this day and discuss at this time. We have discussed and learned a lot about our church. You have called us, Lord, for this church, and we are responsible to sustain it as it was handed to us by the missionaries. Help us to implement what you have called us to do in this church of the Anyuwaa. Bless our works and our ministries and we look forward to meeting again. In Jesus name. Amen."

Discussion Group:

Rev. Darach Thatha Abwola

Qes. Gilo Nyigori Okoth

Pastor Peter Agwa Ochalla

Pastor Omo Okwori Ochudho

Mr. Ojulu Okach

Pastor Agwa Okogn

Pastor Ojulu Omod

Qes Omod Obang Oman

Interviewees:

Rev. Gilo Gora Agwa

Mrs. Apay Okello Olok

Mrs. Olima Ochik Gota

Rev. Oboya Oman Ochalla

Mr. Oman Ogala Oman

Rev. Carl Templin

Bibliography

Achebe, Chinua. *Things Fall Apart*. New York: Anchor, 1994.

Askou100. "Dr Garang's Famous London Address 2nd of March 2002 Part Two." YouTube video, 25:09, Oct 17, 2014. https://www.youtube.com/watch?v=DoDBYEaVVYQ.

Barclay, William. *The Letters to the Philippians, Colossians, and Thessalonians: The Daily Study Bible*. Rev. ed. Philadelphia: Westminster, 1975.

———. *The Letter to the Romans: The Daily Study Bible*. Edinburgh: Saint Andrew, 1960.

Bradshaw, Paul F., et al. "Concerning Confessors." In *The Apostolic Tradition: A Commentary*, edited by Harold W. Attridge, 67–70. Minneapolis: 1517 Media, 2002. https://www.jstor.org/stable/j.ctvb9371z.

Calvin, John. *Institutes of the Christian Religion: 1541 French Edition*. Translated by Elsie Anne Mckee. Grand Rapids: Eerdmans, 2009.

Central Statistics Agency of Ethiopia. *Population and Housing Census 2007—Gambella Statistical*. Addis Ababa, Ethiopia: Central Statistics Agency of Ethiopia, 2007. http://www.statsethiopia.gov.et/wp-content/uploads/2019/06/Population-and-Housing-Census-2007-Gambella_Statistical.pdf.

Christian Families Today. *Living Jesus: Growing in the Life We Were Made to Live*. Newnan, GA: Christian Families Today, 2019.

Dillenberger, John, ed. *Martin Luther: Selection from His Writings*. New York: Anchor, 1962.

"Ethiopia: Crimes Against Humanity in Gambella Region." Human Rights Watch, Mar 23, 2005. https://www.hrw.org/news/2005/03/23/ethiopia-crimes-against-humanity-gambella-region#.

Evans-Pritchard, E. E. *The Political System of the Anuak of the Anglo-Egyptian Sudan.* Oxford: Berg, 2006.

Freedman, David Noel, et al., eds. *Eerdmans Dictionary of the Bible.* Grand Rapids: Eerdmans, 2000.

Gittins, Anthony J. *Reading the Clouds: Mission Spirituality for New Times.* Liguori, MO: Liguori,1999.

Gonzalez, Josto L. *The Story of Christianity: The Early Church to the Dawn of the Reformation.* Vol. 1. New York: HarperCollins, 1984.

Gray, Tim, and Jeff Cavins. *Walking with God: A Journey through the Bible.* West Chester: Ascension, 2009.

Hoekstra, Harvey T. *Honey, We're Going to Africa!* Mukilteo, WA: Wine, 1995.

Jeffers, James S. *The Greco-Roman World of the New Testament Era: Exploring the Background of Early Christianity.* Downer Grove: IVP Academic, 1999.

Kirwan, L. P. "An Ethiopian-Sudanese Frontier Zone in Ancient History." *The Geographical Journal* 138.4, (1972) 457–65.

Kurimoto, Eisei. "Natives and Outsiders: The Historical Experience of the Anywaa of Western Ethiopia." *Journal of Asian and African Studies* 43 (1992) 1–43.

Lewis, C. S. *Mere Christianity: A Revised and Enlarged Edition, with a New Introduction, of the Three Books "The Case for Christianity," "Christians Behaviour," and "Beyond Personality."* New York: Macmillan, 1960.

Lienhardt, Godfrey. "Anuak Village Headmen: II." *Africa: Journal of the International African Institute* 28.1 (1958) 23–36. https://www.jstor.org/stable/1156571.

"Limmud." Bible Hub, n.d. https://biblehub.com/hebrew/3928.htm.

Lindberg, Garter. *The European Reformation.* Malden, MA: Wiley-Blackwell, 2010.

"Make Disciples, Not Just Converts: Evangelism without Discipleship Dispenses Cheap Grace." *Christianity Today* 43.12 (1999) 28–29. https://www.christianitytoday.com/ct/1999/october25/9tc028.html.

Marriner, Keith "Discipleship Lessons from the Old Testament." The International Pentecostal Holiness Church, Oct 7, 2016. https://iphc.org/discipleship/2016/10/07/discipleship-lessons-old-testament/.

"Mathétés." Bible Hub, n.d. https://biblehub.com/greek/3101.htm.

"Menó." Bible hub, n.d. https://biblehub.com/greek/3306.htm.

McClure, W. Donald. *Red-Headed, Rash and Religious: The Story of a Pioneer Missionary.* Edited by Marion Fairman. Indiana, PA: A. G. Halldin, 1954.

McConville, Gordon. "Deuteronomy." In *New Bible Commentary: 21st Century Edition,* edited by Gordon J. Wenham et al., 198–232. Downers Grove: IVP, 2007.

McKenzie, John L. *Dictionary of the Bible.* Milwaukee: Bruce, 1965.

Mullin, Robert Bruce. *A Short World History of Christianity.* Louisville: John Knox, 2008.

Office of Population and Housing Census Commission. *The 1994 Population and Housing Census of Ethiopia: Results for Gambela Region.* Addis Ababa,

Ethiopia: Office of Population and Housing Census Commission, 1994. http://www.statsethiopia.gov.et/wp-content/uploads/2019/06/Population-and-Housing-Census-1994-Gambela-Region.pdf.

Ojulu, Ojob Miru. "The Anyuwaa Traditional Religion and the Bible Preachers." Bachelor of theology essay, Mekane Yesus Theological Seminary, 2002.

Okom, Obang Okumu. "Anyuwaa Traditional Administration and Political Systems." Master's thesis, Argosy University, 2012.

Olupona, Jacob K., ed. *African Spirituality: Forms, Meanings, and Expressions.* New York: Herder, 2000.

Osmer, Richard Robert. *The Teaching Ministry of Congregations.* Louisville: WJK, 2005.

Partee, Charles. *The Story of Don McClure: Adventure in Africa.* Grand Rapids: Zondervan, 1990.

Perner, Conradin. *Anyuak Histories: The Anyuak-Living on Earth in the Sky.* Vol. 8. Basel, Switzerland: Schwabe, 2016.

———. *The Human Territory: The Anyuak-Living on Earth in the Sky.* Vol. 2. Ettenheim, Germany: Helbing & Lichtenhah, 1997.

———. *The Sphere of Spirituality: The Anyuak-Living on Earth in the Sky.* Vol. 1. Basel, Switzerland: Helbing & Lichtenahn, 1994.

Selderhuis, Herman J., ed. *The Calvin Handbook.* Translated by Henry J. Baron et al. Grand Rapids: Eerdmans, 2009.

Shillington, Kevin. *History of Africa.* Rev. ed. New York: St. Martin's, 1995.

Stinton, Diane B. *Jesus of Africa: Voices of Contemporary African Christology Faith and Cultures Series.* Maryknoll: Orbis, 2004.

Stott, John. *The Radical Disciple: Some Neglected Aspects of Our Calling.* Downers Grove: IVP, 2010.

Vanhoozer, Kevin J. *Everyday Theology: How to Read Cultural Texts and Interpret Trends.* Edited by Charles A. Anderson and Michael J. Sleasman. Grand Rapids: Baker Academic. 2007.

———. *Faith Speaking Understanding: Performing the Drama of Doctrine.* Louisville: Westminster John Knox, 2014.

———. *Hearers and Doers: A Pastor's Guide to Make Disciples Through Scripture and Doctrine.* Bellingham, WA: Lexham, 2019.

Wall, L. Lewis. "Anuak Politics, Ecology, and the Origins of Shilluk Kingship." *Ethnology* 15.2 (1976) 151–62.

Watts, John D. W., et al., eds. *Word Biblical Commentary: Isaiah 1–33.* Waco: Word, 1985.

Wax, Trevin K. *Eschatological Discipleship: Leading Christians to Understand Their Historical and Cultural Context.* Nashville: B&H Academic, 2018.

Willard, Dallas. *The Great Omission: Reclaiming Jesus's Essential Teachings on Discipleship.* New York: HarperOne, 2009. Kindle ed.

Zewde, Bahru. "An Overview and Assessment of Gambella Trade (1904–935)." *International Journal of African Historical Studies* 20.1 (1987) 5–94.

———. "'Twixt Sirdar and Emperor: The Anuak in Ethio-Sudanese Relations 1902–1935." *Northeast African Studies* 12.1 (1990) 79–93. http://www.jstor.org/stable/43660301.